# ALTERNATIVE VALUES

# ALTERNATIVE VALUES

*The Perennial Debate about Wealth, Power, Fame, Praise, Glory, and Physical Pleasure*

EDITED WITH AN INTRODUCTION BY HUNTER LEWIS

Axios Press

Axios Press
P.O. Box 118
Mount Jackson, VA 22842

888.542.9467     press@axiosinstitute.org

Acknowledgments and Permissions begin on page 189.


Library of Congress Catalog Control Number:  2003106285

ISBN: 0-9661908-6-6

# CONTENTS

Introduction...................................... ix

**Wealth**......................................... 1

*Arguments against the Pursuit of Wealth*
  Basic Arguments............................1
  Philosophical Arguments ..................10

*Arguments for the Pursuit of Wealth*
  Basic Arguments...........................32
  Philosophical Arguments ..................41

**Power**.......................................... 43

*Arguments against the Pursuit of Power*
  Basic Arguments...........................43
  Philosophical Arguments ..................52

*Arguments for the Pursuit of Power*
  Arguments for the Pursuit of Power in Order to
    Do Good..................................63
  Arguments for the Pursuit of Power in Order to
    Achieve Independence or Defend Oneself....65
  Arguments for the Pursuit of Power for
    Its Own Sake ............................67

**Fame**........................................... 81

*Arguments against the Pursuit of Fame*
  Basic Arguments...........................81
  Philosophical Arguments ..................90

*continued*

*Arguments for the Pursuit of Fame*
    Basic Arguments . . . . . . . . . . . . . . . . . . . . . . . . . . . . .95
    Philosophical Arguments . . . . . . . . . . . . . . . . . .100

## Praise . . . . . . . . . . . . . . . . . . . . . . . . . . . . . . . . . . . . . . 103

*Arguments against the Pursuit of Praise*
    Basic Arguments . . . . . . . . . . . . . . . . . . . . . . . . . . . . .103
    Philosophical Arguments . . . . . . . . . . . . . . . . . .107

*Arguments for the Pursuit of Praise*
    Basic Arguments . . . . . . . . . . . . . . . . . . . . . . . . . . . . .113
    Philosophical Arguments . . . . . . . . . . . . . . . . . .115

## Glory . . . . . . . . . . . . . . . . . . . . . . . . . . . . . . . . . . . . . . . 119

*Arguments against the Pursuit of Glory*
    Basic Arguments . . . . . . . . . . . . . . . . . . . . . . . . . . . . .119
    Philosophical Arguments . . . . . . . . . . . . . . . . . .123

*Arguments for the Pursuit of Glory*
    Basic Arguments . . . . . . . . . . . . . . . . . . . . . . . . . . . . .125
    Philosophical Arguments . . . . . . . . . . . . . . . . . .128

## Pleasure (Physical) . . . . . . . . . . . . . . . . . . . . . . . . . . . 129

### *Sex*

*Arguments against the Free Pursuit of Sex*
    Basic Arguments . . . . . . . . . . . . . . . . . . . . . . . . . . . . .129
    Philosophical Arguments . . . . . . . . . . . . . . . . . .135
    The Special Case of Adultery . . . . . . . . . . . . . . .141

*Arguments for the Free (or Fairly Free) Pursuit of Sex*
    Basic Arguments . . . . . . . . . . . . . . . . . . . . . . . . . . . . .143
    Philosophical Arguments . . . . . . . . . . . . . . . . . .155
    The Special Case of Adultery . . . . . . . . . . . . . . .157

*continued*

## *Drink*

*Arguments against the Free Pursuit of Drink
(or Similar Pleasures)*

 Basic Arguments . . . . . . . . . . . . . . . . . . . . . . . . . . .159

 Philosophical Arguments . . . . . . . . . . . . . . . . . . 162

*Arguments for the Free Pursuit of Drink* . . . . . . . . . .163

## Miscellany . . . . . . . . . . . . . . . . . . . . . . . . . . . . . . . . . . 169

*Arguments against the Pursuit of Wealth and
Power* . . . . . . . . . . . . . . . . . . . . . . . . . . . . . . . . . . . . . . 169

*Arguments for the Pursuit of Wealth and Power* . . . .174

*Arguments against the Pursuit of Wealth and
Fame* . . . . . . . . . . . . . . . . . . . . . . . . . . . . . . . . . . . . . . . .176

*Arguments against the Pursuit of Wealth and
Praise* . . . . . . . . . . . . . . . . . . . . . . . . . . . . . . . . . . . . . . .176

*Arguments against the Pursuit of Wealth, Power,
and Pleasure* . . . . . . . . . . . . . . . . . . . . . . . . . . . . . . . . 177

*Arguments against the Free Pursuit of Sex and
Drink* . . . . . . . . . . . . . . . . . . . . . . . . . . . . . . . . . . . . . . 178

*Arguments for the Free Pursuit of Sex and Drink* . . 179

## Index . . . . . . . . . . . . . . . . . . . . . . . . . . . . . . . . . . . . . . . . 181

# INTRODUCTION

Since we lack inherited instincts of the sort that operate in most animals, we must rely on our value judgments. Hunger impels us to eat, but we learn to judge what is nutritious, not to mention good tasting, and what is not, and we very quickly develop ideas that differ from our parents'.

In this sense, our most fundamental need as an independent organism is to develop values, as fundamental as the need for food, water, and shelter, and ultimately linked in that we cannot have one without the other. Once our basic physical needs are met, we need values all the more, so that we can spring out of bed in the morning with some sense of what we want to do with the day and ultimately with our lives.

Values are so much part of what we are that it can be difficult to objectify or even define them. They are clearly judgments, although the word judgment implies a conscious decision, and values may not be consciously considered or even thought about. At the simplest level, we may think of them as choices, choices that reflect preferences, but also underlying assumptions, attitudes, and beliefs.

In the world in which we find ourselves, there is no shortage of things to like or dislike, to value or devalue, to choose or reject, to choose or reject under some circumstances but not under others. The possibilities are truly infinite. Even trying to categorize the possibilities is fraught with difficulty. Nevertheless one can try to create a manageable list, however tentative, subjective, personal, or unduly abstract it may seem, as in the following.

### *Objects or States of Being Worth Valuing*

- Wealth
- Power
- Fame
- Praise
- Glory
- Pleasure (physical)
- Safety/Health
- Stimulus/Excitement
- Movement
- Appreciation (of the external world)
- Independence
- Accomplishment (for its own sake)
- Order
- Cooperation/Peace
- Love/Community
- Service/Altruism
- Knowledge/Discovery
- Other Worlds (beyond the apparent one)

Looking at this list, it immediately strikes us that the first six are more likely to be for ourselves, although they can also be shared, while the second 12 items are both more likely to be shared and more likely to be enjoyed if shared with others. The first six items should not necessarily be considered selfish desires; one may seek power or wealth, not simply for status or luxury, not for oneself or solely for oneself, but rather to "do good" and "help others" in the world. But the first six necessarily involve the self, and we do commonly want them for ourselves more than for others. Moreover, these six are typically some of our most intense, most passionate desires, and no one can claim that he or she has not been stirred by them at one time or another.

But are these particular desires really desirable? For that matter, is desire itself desirable? Should we let desires rip, especially the passionate desires for wealth, power, pleasure, etc., or should we rein them in, or even try to extirpate them? Strong arguments, some hard and logical, some empirical and well documented, some emotional and quite moving, some deeply and inexpressibly intuitive, have been offered on each side of this debate over the centuries and are assembled in this book. This introduction will just focus on a few of these themes, particularly some of the arguments pro and con desire itself, which underlie all the further arguments pro and con specific desires such as wealth or power or pleasure.

The case for letting desires rip was articulated as soon as people could write:

> Follow your desire as long as you live. . . .
> PTAHHOTPE [c. 2350 B.C.E.], *Maxims of Ptahhotpe*

The person who would truly live ought to allow

personal desires to wax to the uttermost [and] when they have grown to their greatest...have the courage and intelligence to minister to them and satisfy such longings.

PLATO [C. 429–347 B.C.E.], *Gorgias* (Callicles speaking)

The Rule of their Order had but one clause: Do What Thou Wilt.

FRANÇOIS RABELAIS [1494?–1553], *Gargantua and Pantagruel*

Wouldst...live a coward in thine esteem, Letting "I dare not" wait upon "I would," Like the poor cat i' the adage?

WILLIAM SHAKESPEARE [1564–1616], *Macbeth* I, vii

He begins to die, that quits his desires.

GEORGE HERBERT [1593–1633], *Outlandish Proverbs*

To have no desire is to be dead.

THOMAS HOBBES [1588–1679], *Leviathan*

Sooner murder an infant in its cradle than nurse unacted desires....He who desires but acts not, breeds pestilence....Those who restrain desire, do so because theirs is weak enough to be restrained.

WILLIAM BLAKE [1757–1827], *The Marriage of Heaven and Hell*

It seems to me we can never give up longing and wishing while we are thoroughly alive. There are certain things we feel to be beautiful and good, and we must hunger after them.

GEORGE ELIOT (MARY ANN EVANS CROSS) [1819–1880],
*The Mill on the Floss*

What ailed us, O gods, to desert you
For creeds that refuse and restrain?
Come down and redeem us from virtue,
Our Lady of Pain.

ALGERNON CHARLES SWINBURNE [1837–1909],
*Dolores*, st. 35

The natural man has only two primal passions,
to get and to beget.

WILLIAM OSLER [1849–1919], *Science and Immortality*

There are two things to aim at in life: first, to get
what you want; and after that, to enjoy it. Only
the wisest of mankind achieve the second.

LOGAN PEARSALL SMITH [1865–1946], *Afterthoughts*

There is only one big thing—desire. And before
it, when it is big, all is little.

WILLA CATHER [1873–1947], *The Song of the Lark*

My passions were all gathered together like fingers
that made a fist. Drive is considered aggression
today; I knew it then as purpose.

BETTE DAVIS [1908–1989], *The Lonely Life*

I'm going to get it, what's mine.

JIMMY CLIFF [1948– ], *The Harder They Come*

If you want to touch the other shore badly

enough, barring an impossible situation, you will. If your desire is diluted for any reason, you'll never make it.

DIANA NYAD [1949– ], Other Shores

Contentment...cannot signify anything other than the psychological state that exists when the desires of the moment are satisfied.

MORTIMER ADLER [1902–2001], Ten Philosophical Mistakes

Compared to my heart's desire the sea is a drop.

ADÉLIA PRADO [1935– ], Denouement

Our visions begin with our desires.

AUDRE LORDE [1934–1992],<br>In Claudia Tate, Black Women Writers at Work

You can have anything you want if you want it desperately enough. You must want it with an inner exuberance that erupts through the skin and joins the energy that created the world.

SHEILAH GRAHAM [1904–1988], The Rest of the Story

In principle, a person's regrets when death approaches should be affected by all of the important actions left undone [desires not acted on or not acted on successfully]. ... "I never managed to do that," he might think, or "since this was included in my life, I can die content."

ROBERT NOZICK [1938–2002], The Examined Life

If fate should say, "Thy course is run,"
It would not make me sad;
All that I wished to do is done,
All that I would have, had.

LAURENCE HOPE (ADELA CORY FLORENCE NICOLSON)
[1865–1904], *The Court of Pomegranates*

Implicit in all this is an equation of realized or satisfied desires with delight and happiness:

The delight that consumes the desire,
The desire that outruns the delight.

ALGERNON CHARLES SWINBURNE [1837–1909], *Dolores,* st. 14

Continual success in obtaining those things which a man from time to time desireth, that is to say, continual prospering, is that men call felicity. . . .

THOMAS HOBBES [1588–1679], *Leviathan*

Justice is noblest, and health is best,
But the heart's desire is the pleasantest.

Inscription at Delos,
Quoted by ARISTOTLE [384–322 B.C.E.]
in *The Nicomachean Ethics*

Ah love! could you and I with Him conspire
To grasp this sorry scheme of things entire,
Would not we shatter it to bits—and then
Re-mold it nearer to the heart's desire!

EDWARD FITZGERALD [1809–1883],
*Rubáiyát of Omar Khayyám*

Even the recollection of failed desires may rob us of happiness:

> When to the sessions of sweet silent thought
> I summon up remembrance of things past,
> I sigh the lack of many a thing I sought,
> And with old woes new wail my dear times' waste.
>
> WILLIAM SHAKESPEARE [1564–1616], *Sonnets*

Of course, not everyone equates satisfied desire with happiness, or even thinks that happiness is itself desirable. In 1992, Dr. Richard Bentall, senior clinical psychology lecturer at Liverpool University in England, published a report titled: "A Proposal to Classify Happiness as a Psychological Disorder." The report, which was evidently not written tongue in cheek, stated that:

> Happy people are less rational than depressed people. Depressed people are better judges of what people think about them. ... There is consistent evidence that happy people overestimate their control over environmental events, often to the point of perceiving completely random events as subject to their will.

In reading Dr. Bentall, one is reminded of the crucial role that terminology plays in any discussion of values: does he mean what most people mean by happiness, or is he really referring to mania, very often confused with happiness by people gripped by mania, but surely a faux-happiness at best?

In any case, there are legions of people who do value happiness highly, but who do not believe that letting desires rip is any way to realize it. For one thing, the odds may be against realizing the desire or the desire may turn out badly:

> There is not a fiercer hell than the failure in a great object.
>
> JOHN KEATS [1795–1821], *Endymion*

> These violent delights have violent ends.
>
> WILLIAM SHAKESPEARE [1564–1616], *Romeo and Juliet* II, vi

> Desire can blind us to the hazards of our enterprises.
>
> MARIE DE FRANCE [1155–1190],
> *Medieval Fables of Marie de France*

Sometimes the outcome is ambiguous:

> The desires of the heart are as crooked as corkscrews. . . .
>
> W(YSTAN) H(UGH) AUDEN [1907–1973], *Death's Echo*

> We would often be sorry if our wishes were gratified.
>
> AESOP [C. 620–C. 560 B.C.E.], *The Old Man and Death*

> When the gods wish to punish us they answer our prayers.
>
> OSCAR (FINGALL O'FLAHERTIE WILLS) WILDE [1854–1900],
> *An Ideal Husband*

> In this world there are only two tragedies. One is not getting what one wants, and the other is

getting it.

> OSCAR (FINGALL O'FLAHERTIE WILLS) WILDE [1854–1900],
> *Lady Windemere's Fan,* Act II

We, ignorant of ourselves,
Beg often our own harms, which the wise powers
Deny us for our good; so find we profit
By losing of our prayers.

> WILLIAM SHAKESPEARE [1564–1616],
> *Antony and Cleopatra* II, i

Protect me from what I want.

> JENNY HOLZER [1950– ], *Truisms*

E'en crosses from his sov'reign hand
Are blessings in disguise.

> JAMES HERVEY [1714–1758],
> *Reflections on a Flower-Garden*

Life is made up of desires that seem big and vital
one minute, and little and absurd the next. I guess
we get what's best for us in the end.

> ALICE CALDWELL RICE [1870–1942],
> *A Romance of Billy-Goat Hill*

Sometimes, in retrospect, the effort seems quite out of
proportion to the gain:

> 'Tis an old lesson; time approves it true,
> And those who know it best, deplore it most;
> When all is won that all desire to woo,
> The paltry prize is hardly worth the cost.

> GEORGE NOEL GORDON, LORD BYRON [1788–1824],
> *Childe Harold*

If not out of proportion to the gain, the effort can still be considerable:

> For you to be successful, sacrifices must be made. It's better that they are made by others but failing that, you'll have to make them yourself.
>
> RITA MAE BROWN [1944– ], *Starting From Scratch*

> We all must pay with the current coin of life
> For the honey that we taste.
>
> RACHEL (BLUWSTEIN) [1890–1931], *Collected Poems*

> I do not know anyone who has got to the top without hard work. That is the recipe. It will not always get you to the top, but it should get you pretty near.
>
> MARGARET THATCHER [1925– ],
> quoted in London *Daily Telegraph*

There is also a problem of timing. The gain may arrive too late:

> Most men that do thrive in the world do forget to take pleasure during the time that they are getting their estate, but reserve that till they have got one, and then it is too late for them to enjoy it.
>
> SAMUEL PEPYS [1633–1703], *Diary*

Sometimes we succeed, only to stumble:

> When a man's knowledge is sufficient to attain, and his virtue is not sufficient to enable him to hold, whatever he may have gained, he will lose

again.

CONFUCIUS [551–479 B.C.E.], *Analects*

In any case:

The top is not forever. Either you walk down,
or you are going to be kicked down.

JANET COLLINS [1917– ], in Brian Lanker, *I Dream a
World: Portraits of Black Women Who Changed America*

And:

No list of successes can bestow so much happiness
as their diminution will cause annoyance.

MARCUS TULLIUS CICERO [106–43 B.C.E.], *Disputations*

Ultimately of course, no one holds on to anything:

But is there any comfort to be found?
Man is in love and loves what vanishes,
What more is there to say?

WILLIAM BUTLER YEATS [1865–1939],
*The Tower Nineteen Hundred and Nineteen*, I, st. 6

Desire himself runs out of breath,
And getting, doth but gain his death.

WALTER ALEXANDER RALEIGH [1861–1922],
"Affection is Not Love"

Renunciation is submission to time.

SIMONE WEIL [1909–1943],
*The Notebooks of Simone Weil*

Moreover, desire may grow so immoderately, so uncontrollably, that it becomes disturbing. As Montaigne wrote:

> I would feel it come to life, grow, and increase in spite of my resistance, and finally seize me, alive and watching, and possess me, to such an extent that, as from drunkenness, the picture of things began to seem to me other than usual. I would see the advantages of the object of my desire visibly expanding and growing, increasing and swelling from the breath of my imagination; the difficulties of my undertaking growing easy and smooth, my reason and my conscience withdrawing.
>
> MICHEL EYQUEM DE MONTAIGNE [1533–1592], *Essays*, II, 12, "Apology for Raymond Sebond"

Swelling passions may transmogrify into vipers:

> Every desire is a viper in the bosom, who, while he was chill, was harmless; but when warmth gave him strength exerted it in poison.
>
> SAMUEL JOHNSON [1709–1784], Letter to James Boswell

Or burst into flame:

> Pain wanders through my bones like a lost fire.
> What burns me now?
> Desire, desire, desire.
>
> THEODORE ROETHKE [1908–1963], *The Marrow*

Or end in conflagration:

> Some say the world will end in fire,
> Some say in ice.

From what I've tasted of desire
I hold with those who favor fire.

ROBERT FROST [1874–1963], "Fire and Ice"

Desire may only provoke boredom:

It is almost as easy to be enervated by triumph
as by defeat.

MAX LERNER [1902–1992], *Actions and Passions*

Unless a man has been taught what to do with
success after getting it, the achievement of it must
inevitably leave him a prey to boredom.

BERTRAND RUSSELL [1872–1970],
*The Conquest of Happiness*

But more commonly involves darker emotions of fear or
anxiety:

From craving arises sorrow and from craving
arises fear.

BUDDHA (SIDDHARTHA GAUTAMA) [C. 563–483 B.C.E.],
*Dhammapada*

No man is so completely happy that something
somewhere does not clash with his condition. It
is the nature of human affairs to be fraught with
anxiety; they never prosper perfectly and they
never remain constant.

(ANCIUS MANLIUS SEVERINUS) BOETHIUS [C. 480–525],
*The Consolation of Philosophy*

Remember, too, that all the most happy men are
over-sensitive. They have never experienced adversity

and so unless everything obeys their slightest whim they are prostrated by every minor upset. . . .

*Ibid.*

The technique of winning is so shoddy, the terms of winning are so ignoble, the tenure of winning is so brief; and the specter of the has-been—a shameful rather than a pitiable sight today—brings a sudden chill even to our sunlit moments.

LOUIS KRONENBERGER [1904–1980], *Company Manners*

Why are things so terribly, unbearably precious that you can't enjoy them but can only wait breathless in dread of their going?

ANNE MORROW LINDBERGH [1906–2001],
*Hour of Gold, Hour of Lead*

Most successes are unhappy. That's why they are successes—they have to reassure themselves about themselves by achieving something that the world will notice. . . . The happy people are failures because they are on such good terms with themselves that they don't give a damn.

AGATHA CHRISTIE [1891–1976], *Remembered Death*

Desire may also provoke anger:

He . . . hates himself, because in his sickness he knows not the cause of his malady.

LUCRETIUS (TITUS LUCRETIUS CARUS) [99–55 B.C.E.],
*On the Nature of Things*

Or sorrow:

> Consume my heart away; sick with desire
> And fastened to a dying animal
> It knows not what it is; and gather me
> Into the artifice of eternity.
>
> WILLIAM BUTLER YEATS [1865–1939], *Sailing to Byzantium*

Aristotle generally thought well enough of desire:

> That which all desire is good, as we have said, and
> so, the more a thing is desired the better it is.
>
> ARISTOTLE [384–322 B.C.E.], *Rhetoric*

But he also agreed with Plato's assertion that:

> Desires are unbounded.
>
> PLATO [c. 429–347 B.C.E.], *Laws*, XI

And elaborated by noting that:

> The avarice of mankind is insatiable; at one time
> two obols was pay enough; but now, when this
> sum has become customary, men always want
> more and more without end; for it is of the nature
> of desire not to be satisfied, and most men live
> only for the gratification of it.
>
> ARISTOTLE [384–322 B.C.E.], *Politics*

Even growing rich settles little:

> It almost always happens that the man who grows
> rich changes his notions of poverty. . . .
>
> SAMUEL JOHNSON [1709–1784], *The Rambler*

To be content with little is hard, to be content with much, impossible.

MARIE VON EBNER-ESCHENBACH [1830–1916], *Aphorisms*

Moreover:

If a man pursues wealth by trying to avoid poverty, he is not working to get power; he prefers being unknown and unrecognized, and even denies himself many natural pleasures to avoid losing the money he has got. But certainly no sufficiency is achieved this way, since he is lacking in power and vexed by trouble.... And if a man pursues only power, he expends wealth, despises pleasures and honour without power, and holds glory of no account. But you can see how much this man also lacks; at any one time he lacks the necessaries of life and is consumed by worry, from which he cannot free himself, so he ceases to be what he most of all wants to be, that is, powerful. A similar argument can be applied to honour, glory, and pleasures, for, since any one of them is the same as the others, a man who pursues one of them to the exclusion of the others, cannot even acquire the one he wants.

(ANCIUS MANLIUS SEVERINUS) BOETHIUS [c. 480–525], *The Consolation of Philosophy*

In any case:

The act of longing for something will always be more intense than the requiting of it.

GAIL GODWIN [1937– ], *Dream Children*

> All things that are,
> Are with more spirit chased than enjoy'd.
>
> WILLIAM SHAKESPEARE [1564–1616],
> *The Merchant of Venice* II, vi

And:

> For it so falls out
> That what we have we prize not to the worth
> Whiles we enjoy it, but being lack'd and lost,
> Why, then we rack the value, then we find
> The virtue that possession would not show us
> Whiles it was ours.
>
> WILLIAM SHAKESPEARE [1564–1616],
> *Much Ado About Nothing* IV, i

And:

> In the morning thou shalt say, Would God it were
> even! and at even thou shalt say, Would God it
> were morning!
>
> *Deuteronomy* 28:67

To which Lucretius added that:

> Whilst what we crave is wanting, it seems to
> transcend all the rest; then, when it has been
> gotten, we crave something else, and ever does
> the same thirst of life possess us, as we gape for
> it open-mouthed.
>
> LUCRETIUS (TITUS LUCRETIUS CARUS) [99–55 B.C.E.],
> *On the Nature of Things*, III

The man who is tired of staying at home, often

goes out abroad from his great mansion, and of a sudden returns again, for indeed abroad he feels no better. He races to his country home, furiously driving his ponies, as though he were hurrying to bring help to a burning house. He yawns at once, when he has set foot on the threshold of the villa, or sinks into a heavy sleep and seeks forgetfulness, or even in hot haste makes for town, eager to be back.

Ibid.

Bette Davis further added:

I am doomed to an eternity of compulsive work. No set goal achieved satisfies. Success only breeds a new goal. The golden apple devoured has seeds. It is endless.

BETTE DAVIS [1908–1989], *The Lonely Life*

For, as Pliny said:

An object in possession seldom retains the same charm that it had in pursuit.

PLINY THE YOUNGER (GAIUS PLINIUS CAECILLIUS SECUNDUS) [c. 61–c. 114], *Letters*

Which leads to Horace's conclusion that:

We rarely find anyone who can say he has lived a happy life, and who, content with his life, can retire from the world like a satisfied guest.

HORACE (QUINTUS HORATIUS FLACCUS) [65–8 B.C.E.], *Satires*

Such unlimited demands easily tip over into chronic misery, as Locke described:

> That desire is a state of uneasiness, everyone who reflects on himself will quickly find.... Life itself, and all its enjoyments, is a burden cannot be borne under the lasting and unremoved pressure of such an uneasiness.
>
> JOHN LOCKE [1632–1704],
> *Concerning Human Understanding,* Book II, XXI, 32

Lao-tzu agrees that:

> There is no calamity greater than out-of-control desires.
>
> LAO-TZU [c. 604–531 B.C.E.], *The Way of Lao-tzu*

The essential problem is that:

> The five blessings are long life, riches, serenity, the love of virtue, and the attainment of ambition.
>
> *The Hung-Fan* [1100 B.C.E.]

but the five are largely incompatible, especially serenity with either riches or ambition.

Among those who are skeptical of desire, or at least wish to rein it in a bit, there is not necessarily uniformity of view. The most prevalent notion is that desire, being an emotion,* can and should be governed by reason:

---

\* Whether desire actually is an emotion is debated among psychologists. This author believes it is not only an emotion, it is one of the five "basic" emotions along with fear, sadness, anger, and happiness, as argued in *The Beguiling Serpent.*

Rule your desires lest your desires rule you.

PUBLILIUS SYRUS [C. 100 B.C.E.], *Sententiae*

But, from that point, the agreement ends. For example, the reliance on reason to manage emotion can lead to the highest unselfishness, as in Kantian ethics, or in Albert Einstein's personal philosophy:

> A person who is religiously enlightened appears to me to be one who has, to the best of his ability, liberated himself from the fetters of his selfish desires and is preoccupied with thoughts, feelings, and aspirations to which he clings because of their superpersonal value.
>
> ALBERT EINSTEIN [1879–1955],
> quoted in Lewis, *A Question of Values*

Contrarily, reason can be used for less unselfish ends, as in the "rational–emotive" therapy of psychologist Albert Ellis:

> Your paramount absorption should unashamedly be the fulfillment of your own desires, your morality that of enlightened self-interest and unabashed individualism.
>
> The sane and truly enlightened individualist however, will not define his desires as demands, nor his preferences as needs....And he will be lovingly devoted, in most instances, to selected other people because through such intimate relationships he can more fully know and enjoy himself.
>
> ALBERT ELLIS [1913– ], *A Guide to Rational Living*

Beyond the question of whether reason should reduce or simply refine the selfishness of many of our desires, there is a further question of whether reason should reduce or refine the desires themselves. Proponents of reducing desires argue that one should:

> Manifest plainness,
> Embrace simplicity,
> Reduce selfishness,
> Have few desires.
>
> LAO-TZU [c. 604–531 B.C.E.], *The Way of Lao-tzu*

And:

> If you want to make Pythocles happy do not augment his wealth but diminish his desires.
>
> EPICURUS [341–270 B.C.E.], *Aphorisms*

Because:

> Nothing troubles you which you do not desire.
>
> MARCUS TULLIUS CICERO [106–43 B.C.E.], *De Senectute*

Montaigne paraphrases Epicurus in taking the position that, if we do not reduce our desires, we should at least look at them in a more realistic light:

> Desires are either natural and necessary, like eating and drinking; or natural and not necessary, like [sexual] intercourse . . . ; or neither natural nor necessary. Of this last type are nearly all those of

men; they are all superfluous and artificial.

MICHEL EYQUEM DE MONTAIGNE [1533–1592], *Essays* II, 12,
"Apology for Raymond Sebond"

Robert Nozick gently disagrees. Rather then reducing our desires, or at least looking at them more realistically, we should consider the possibility of transcending them:

> . . . In the moments I am describing, these other desires—for more money, or another job or another chocolate bar—simply are not operating. . . . There is no additional thing you want right then…your satisfaction is complete. The feeling that accompanies this is intense joy. . . . But we don't find it helpful to be told to first get rid of our existing wants as a way of reaching the state of not wanting anything else. (And this is not simply because we doubt this route leads to an accompanying joy.) Rather, what we want is to be told of something so good, whose nature is so complete and satisfying, that reaching it will exclude any further wants from crowding in, and we want to be told how to reach this.
>
> ROBERT NOZICK [1938–2002], *The Examined Life*

Perhaps the most prevalent rationalist technique for controlling our desires is not to reduce or transcend them but rather to embrace all of them while simultaneously trying to de-intensify them, trying to downshift passionate demands into something more akin to preferences. Santayana expresses this pragmatic approach:

> It is a new road to happiness, if you have strength
> enough to castigate a little the various impulses
> that sway you in turn.
>
> GEORGE SANTAYANA [1863–1952], *Winds of Doctrine*

Epicurus lectures a bit more sternly that pleasure must usually be rescued from the ruin of our own willfulness:

> We should not spoil what we have by desiring
> what we have not, but remember that what we
> have too was the gift of fortune.
>
> EPICURUS [341–270 B.C.E.], *Vatican Sayings*

And also:

> ... We say that pleasure is the objective, [but the
> truest] pleasure [is] the absence of pain in the
> body and of turmoil in the mind.
>
> EPICURUS [341–270 B.C.E.], *Letter to Menoeceus*

A rational attempt to tone down the intensity of desires need not necessarily require a disavowal of more worldly pleasures. The ancient Roman stoic philosopher Seneca warned that:

> Nothing, to the wise man, is a necessity;
>
> LUCIUS ANNAEUS SENECA [55 B.C.E.–c. 39], Letter 9

and that:

> Even the wealthy and the well provided are
> continually met and frustrated by difficult times

and situations. It is in no man's power to have whatever he wants. ...

Ibid., Letter 123

But Seneca was himself one of the wealthiest men of his time, perhaps the wealthiest apart from the Emperor, and he stated forthrightly that:

> I am not, mind you, against your possessing [riches], but I want to ensure that you possess them without tremors. ...

Ibid., Letter 18

He added, in a similar vein, that one should be:

> ...Able to do without friends, not...desire to do without them

Ibid., Letter 9

and also that:

> It is a great man [who] can treat his earthenware as if it [were] silver, [but] a man who treats his silver as if it [were] earthenware is no less great.

Ibid., Letter 5

The modern psychiatrist Karen Horney captured some of this same spirit when she warned that:

> ...A check on wishes...means putting a lid on our aliveness.

KAREN HORNEY [1885–1952],<br>*Human Growth and Neurosis*

But also acknowledged that:

> Resignation may have a constructive meaning. We can think of many older people who have recognized the intrinsic futility of ambition and success, who have mellowed by expecting and demanding less, and who through renunciation of nonessentials have become wiser.
>
> Ibid.

Colette added:

> I love my past. I love my present. I'm not ashamed of what I've had, and I'm not sad because I have it no longer.
>
> (SIDONIE GABRIELLE) COLETTE [1873–1954],<br>*The Last of Cheri*

Neither Seneca nor Horney saw this process as anything but bumpy. As Socrates said:

> In every one of us there are two guiding and ruling principles which lead us whither they will; one is the natural desire of pleasure, the other is an acquired opinion . . . ; and these two are sometimes in harmony and then again at war, and sometimes the one, sometimes the other conquers.
>
> PLATO [c. 429–347 B.C.E.], *Phaedrus*

Just as often, the warfare is more intense:

> Ah, when to the heart of man

> Was it ever less than a treason
> To go with the drift of things,
> To yield with a grace to reason,
> And bow and accept the end
> Of a love or a season?
>
> ROBERT FROST [1874–1963], "Reluctance," st. 4

It may be a struggle:

> I count him braver who overcomes his desires
> than him who conquers his enemies; for the
> hardest victory is the victory over self.
>
> ARISTOTLE [384–322 B.C.E.], quoted in
> Stobaeus, *Floritegium*

But, withal, there is the assumption that reason can prevail, because:

> ...Our life is the creation of our mind.
>
> BUDDHA (SIDDHARTHA GAUTAMA) [c. 563–483 B.C.E.],
> *Dhammapada*

> ...Desire is consequent on opinion rather than
> opinion on desire; for the thinking is the starting
> point.
>
> ARISTOTLE [384–422 B.C.E.], *Metaphysics*

> The wise man is little inconvenienced by fortune:
> things that matter are under the control of his
> own judgement and reason.
>
> EPICURUS [341–270 B.C.E.], *Quotations* in Cicero's works

> Man is not disturbed about things, but by his

opinion about things.

EPICTETUS [55–135], *Handbook*, 5

Why then do you mortal men seek after happiness outside yourselves, when it lies within you?

(ANCIUS MANLIUS SEVERINUS) BOETHIUS [c. 480–525], *The Consolation of Philosophy*

... Nothing is miserable except when you think it so, and vice versa, all luck is good luck to the man who bears it with equanimity.

Ibid.

... There is nothing either good or bad, but thinking makes it so.

WILLIAM SHAKESPEARE [1564–1616], *Hamlet* II, ii

We do not desire a thing because we adjudge it to be good, but, on the contrary, we call it good because we desire it, and consequently everything to which we are averse we call evil. Each person, therefore, according to his affect judges or estimates what is good and what is evil, what is better and what is worse, and what is the best and what is the worst.

BARUCH SPINOZA [1632–1677], *Ethics*

These observations in turn underlie the various forms of cognitive psychology that developed in the twentieth century.

So far we have explored rational methods of managing desires that can be broadly characterized as permissive, that is, methods which are more concerned with the consequences of desires than the desires themselves. But, of course, many, many thinkers find fault with the desires themselves. For example, Seneca's fellow stoic, Epictetus, did not agree at all that pursuing wealth is just fine so long as it does not lead to "tremors":

> There is no profit from the things which are valued and eagerly sought to those who have obtained them; and to those who have not yet obtained them there is an imagination that when these things are come, all that is good will come with them; then, when they are come, the feverish feeling is the same, the tossing to and fro is the same, the satiety, the desire of things which are not present; for freedom is acquired not by the full possession of the things which are desired, but by removing the desire.
>
> EPICTETUS [55–135], *Discourse*, IV, 1

Therefore:

> Do not ask things to happen as you wish, but wish them to happen as they do happen, and your life will go smoothly.
>
> EPICTETUS [55–135] , *Handbook 8*

Epictetus reaches his conclusions through a combination of empiricism (sense experience) and logic. The seventeenth-century philosopher Spinoza reached similar conclusions drawing on empiricism to some extent, but as far as possible, on logic alone:

[From the beginning] I ... [observed that] ... the ordinary surroundings of life which are esteemed by men (as their actions testify) to be the highest good may be classed under the three heads— Riches, Fame, and the Pleasures of Sense: with these three the mind is so absorbed that it has little power to reflect on any different good. By sensual pleasure the mind is enthralled ... so that it is quite incapable of thinking of any other object; when such pleasure has been gratified it is followed by extreme melancholy. ... The pursuit of honors and riches is likewise very absorbing, especially if such objects be sought simply for their own sake. ... In the case of fame the mind is still more absorbed, for fame is conceived as always good for its own sake, and as the ultimate end to which all actions are directed. Further the attainment of riches and fame is not followed as in the case of sensual pleasure by repentance, but, the more we acquire, the greater is our delight, and consequently, the more we are incited to increase both the one and the other; on the other hand, if our hopes happen to be frustrated we are plunged into the deepest sadness. Fame has the further drawback that it compels its votaries to order their lives according to the opinions of their fellow men, shunning what they usually shun, and seeking what they usually seek.

When I saw that all these ordinary objects of desire would be obstacles in the way of a search for something different and new—no, that they were so opposed thereto that either they or it would have to be abandoned, I was forced to inquire which would prove the most useful to me. But further reflection convinced me that ... evils arise from the love of what is perishable, such as the objects already mentioned [while] love toward a thing eternal and infinite feeds the mind wholly with joy, and is itself unmingled with any sadness, wherefore it is greatly to be desired and sought for with all our strength.

BARUCH SPINOZA [1632–1677],
*On the Improvement of the Understanding*

Lao-tzu reached similar conclusions relying primarily on intuition:

To be constantly without desire is the way to have a vision of the mystery (of heaven and earth). ...

LAO-TZU [c. 604–531 B.C.E.], *Tao Te Ching*

Henry David Thoreau, both an empiricist and intuitionist, would presumably have approved of Epictetus', Spinoza's, and Lao-tzu's style of philosophizing as well as their conclusions:

There are nowadays professors of philosophy, but not philosophers. ... To be a philosopher is not merely to have subtle thoughts, nor even to found a school, but so to love wisdom as to live according to its dictates, a life of simplicity, independence, magnanimity, and trust. It is to solve some of the problems of life, not only theoretically, but practically.

HENRY DAVID THOREAU [1817–1862], *Walden*

If such simplicity seems lacking in glory, then so be it:

There are people who live lives little different than the beasts, and I don't mean that badly. I mean that they accept whatever happens day to day without struggle or question or regret. To them things just are, like the earth and sky and seasons.

CELESTE DE BLASIS [1946– ], *Wild Swan*

I am beginning to learn that it is the sweet, simple things of life which are the real ones after all.

LAURA INGALLS WILDER [1867–1957],
in Lorraine Anderson, ed., *Sisters of the Earth*

Buddhism is commonly regarded as a mystical religion, like Taoism drawing upon the inner wellsprings of intuition, but its founder actually relied heavily on empiricism, along with some logic and intuition, to develop his case against having desires (or for that matter aversions) at all:

... If the roots of craving are not wholly uprooted sorrows will come again and again.

BUDDHA (SIDDHARTHA GAUTAMA) [c. 563–483 B.C.E.],
*Dhammapada*

But whoever in this world overcomes his selfish cravings, his sorrows fall away from him, like drops of water from a lotus flower.

Ibid.

Yellow leaves hang on your tree of life. The messengers of death are waiting. You are going to travel far away. Have you any provision for the journey?...You are at the end of your life. You are going to meet Death. There is no resting-place on your way, and you have no provision for the journey....Let a wise man remove impurities from himself even as a silversmith removes impurities from the silver: one after one, little by little, again and again.

Ibid.

The hunger of passions is the greatest disease. Disharmony is the greatest sorrow. When you know this well, then you know that Nirvana is the greatest joy.

Ibid.

He who like the moon is pure, bright, clear and serene; whose pleasure for things that pass away is gone—him I call a Brahmin.

Ibid.

The detachment preached by original Buddhism has been characterized and arguably mischaracterized in many ways. Gerald G. May, for example, has written that:

[Buddhist-inspired] detachment...seeks a liberation of desire, an enhancement of passion, the freedom

> to love with all one's being, and the willingness
> to bear the pain such love can bring.
>
> GERALD G. MAY, Addiction and Grace

This seems an almost willful misreading, but perhaps no worse than the common characterization of Buddhism as pessimistic, world-weary, passive, even immobilized. One of the premises of original Buddhism is that the abandonment of desire and aversion will actually create vitality and joy by liberating energy:

> O let us live in joy, although having nothing! In joy let us live like spirits of light!
>
> BUDDHA (SIDDHARTHA GAUTAMA) [c. 563–483 B.C.E.],<br>Dhammapada

> When desires go, joy comes: the follower of Buddha finds this truth.
>
> Ibid.

Albert Einstein echoes these words:

> I am happy because I want nothing from anyone. I do not care for money. Decorations, titles, or distinctions mean nothing to me. I do not crave praise.
>
> ALBERT EINSTEIN [1879–1955],<br>quoted in Lewis, A Question of Values

Einstein was certainly neither inactive nor passive in nature. As S. N. Goenka, a practitioner of Vipassana Buddhism, perhaps the most faithful contemporary expression of the Buddha's original vision, explains:

> You must act. Life is for action; you should not become inactive. But the action should be performed with...equanimity....If you maintain equanimity, you are certainly progressing on the path. You are breaking the old mental habit of reaction.
>
> S(ATYA) N(ARAYAN) GOENKA [1924– ], *The Art of Living*

The *Bhagavad Gita*, one of the most sacred texts of Hinduism, emphasizes the ideal of an especially vigorous involvement in life, but at the same time a completely detached form of action, an equilibrium even in the midst of the storm, and a complete acceptance of whatever comes:

> ...Get up with a determination to fight, O Arjuna....Do your duty to the best of your ability, O Arjuna, with your mind attached to the Lord, abandoning (worry and) attachment to the results, and remaining calm in both success and failure. The equanimity of mind is called Karmayoga....Those who are not attached to anything, who are neither elated by getting desired results nor troubled by undesired results, their Wisdom is deemed steady.
>
> *Bhagavad Gita* [250 B.C.E.–250] 2:37, 48, 57

As a hard rationalist, that is, someone who especially favored logic, the economist and philosopher Ludwig von Mises was one of those who missed the empiricism imbedded in Buddhism and other elements of ancient Eastern thought. He assumed, somewhat illogically, that the only alternative to a hearty embrace of desire is "inactivity," "resignation," "lethargy," and ultimately "death." However, even von Mises recognized the limits of rationality in thinking about human values. In *Human Action*, he acknowledged that it is neither rational nor irrational to want to be

> As rich as Croesus or as poor as a Buddhist monk.
>
> LUDWIG VON MISES [1881–1973],<br>*Human Action*

precisely because rationality can more readily advise us on means than on the ultimate ends we choose for our lives.

Beyond the limits of rationality, there are of course numerous religious critiques of the human tendency to desire, critiques drawn either from inner intuition or from various forms of revealed authority. Jesus taught unequivocally that wealth, power, fame, praise, glory, and physical pleasure were completely false idols, not just proper goals that, if mishandled, can cause us painful "tremors":

> If any man will come after me, let him deny himself, and take up his cross, and follow me. For whosoever will save his life shall lose it: and whosoever will lose his life for my sake shall

find it.

JESUS [C.4 B.C.E.–30], *Matthew* 16:24-25

Which is echoed by:

We only possess what we renounce; what we
do not renounce escapes from us.

SIMONE WEIL [1909–1943], *Gravity and Grace*

And on a lighter note:

I like to go to Marshall Field's in Chicago just to
see how many things there are in the world that
I do not want.

MOTHER MARY MADELEVA [1887–1964],
*My First Seventy Years*

Although one must be careful: too much spiritual "success" can also be a temptation:

God has not called me to be successful; he has
called me to be faithful.

MOTHER TERESA (AGNES GONXNA BOJAXHIU) [1910–1997],
quoted in the *New York Times*

Puritanism, usually religious but sometimes secular, views
life as a constant struggle against temptation:

When they were got out of the wilderness, they
presently saw a town before them, and the name
of that town is Vanity; and at that town there is a
fair kept, called Vanity Fair. At this fair are all such
merchandise sold as houses, lands, trades, places,
honors, preferments, titles, countries, kingdoms,

lusts, pleasures and delights of all sorts, as whores, bawds, wives, husbands, children, masters, servants, lives, bloods, bodies, souls, silver, gold, pearls, precious stones, and what not.

JOHN BUNYAN [1628–1688], *Pilgrim's Progress*

Religious strictures are thus vitally necessary:

You ask, Why then did God give to all men so many commandments. . . . Since, however, no one is by nature Christian or pious, but every one sinful and evil, God places the restraints of the law upon them all, so that they may not dare give rein to their desires and commit outward, wicked deeds.

MARTIN LUTHER [1483–1546],
"On Secular Authority"

St. Augustine offered a gentler and simpler view:

Love [God] and do what you will.

ST. AUGUSTINE [354–430],
*Tractatus in Epistolam Ioannis ad Parthos*, 7:8

Which will in turn lead to:

. . . Fewer desires, . . . more peace.

THOMAS WILSON [1927–2001],
*Maxims of Piety and Christianity*

This conscious turning away from all desire and aversion naturally has its unstinting critics:

The doctrine that maintains that what I cannot have I must teach myself not to desire; that a desire eliminated, or successfully resisted, is as good as a desire satisfied, seems to me a sublime, but unmistakable, form of the doctrine of sour grapes: what I cannot be sure of, I cannot truly want.

ISAIAH BERLIN [1909–1997], *Two Concepts of Liberty*,
Inaugural Lecture

The stoical scheme of supplying our Wants, by lopping off our Desires, is like cutting off our Feet when we want Shoes.

JONATHAN SWIFT [1667–1745],
*Thoughts of Various Subjects*

There are a set of religions, or rather moral writings, which teach that virtue is the certain road to happiness, and vice to misery, in this world. A very wholesome and comfortable doctrine, and to which we have but one objection, namely, that it is not true.

HENRY FIELDING [1707–1754], *Tom Jones*

By annihilating the desire, you annihilate the mind. Every man without passions has within him no principle of action, nor motive to act.

CLAUDE-ADRIEN HELVÉTIUS [1715–1771], *De l'Esprit*

I think the proverb… "*In medio tutissimus ibis*, Thou will go most safely by taking the middle course,*" is one of the most mischievous, one of the most pernicious, one of the most foolish that ever was invented in the world. I believe very strongly in extremes; and I am quite sure that all progress in the world, whether literary, or scientific, or religious, or political, or social, has been obtained only with the assistance of extremes.

LAFCADIO HEARN [1850–1904],
Lecture, University of Tokyo

In my experience, there is only one motivation, and that is desire. No reasons or principles contain it or stand against it.

JANE SMILEY [1949– ], *Ordinary Love*

Contempt for Riches [is a] False Virtue.

JEREMY BENTHAM [1748–1832], *Deontology*

All progress is based upon a universal innate desire on the part of every organism to live beyond its income.

SAMUEL BUTLER [1612–1680], *Note Books*

Life itself is but motion, and can never be without desire, nor without fear, no more than without sense.

THOMAS HOBBES [1588–1679], *Leviathan*

Our desire must be like a slow and stately ship, sailing across endless oceans, never in search of safe anchorage. Then suddenly, unexpectedly, it will find mooring for a moment.

ETTY HILLESUM [1914–1943],
*An Interrupted Life: The Diaries of Etty Hillesum*

> Not a single act here [below] appears ever to be
> done by a man free from desire; whatever [man]
> does, it is [the result of] the impulse of desire.
>
> MANU [c. 1200 B.C.E.], *Code of Manu*

Jungian psychologist James Hillman argues that the attempt to distance oneself from desire has created:

> An age of sociopathy,
>
> JAMES HILLMAN [1926],
> *A Blue Fire: Selected Writings of James Hillman*

and that in general:

> Spiritual disciplines are part of the disaster of
> the world.
>
> Ibid.

Well, no two people will ever quite agree, which is why each of us must make up his or her mind. Moreover, every ethical question has layers, depths, and nuances that are not easily captured. For example, if one decides that the desire for money is largely a snare and an illusion, does that mean that one should ignore it entirely, even if one then has to depend entirely on the charity of others, like a mendicant Buddhist monk? If such a stance is adopted, is it an example of independence or dependence, and is dependence a sound ethical position?

The purpose of this book is therefore not to try to resolve these problems, but to help each of us sort through them and reach some personal conclusions, however tentative, especially about the most common desires, notably the desire for wealth, power, fame, praise, glory, and physical pleasure. The passages selected are only a sampling of what people have written about these topics over the centuries, both men and women, although any compilation of this kind is frustrated by the fact that women have only recently achieved equality in printed work, and then not in all parts of the world. But whatever their limitations, we hope that the thoughts included will stimulate further thinking and prove useful.

The passages are set up as a kind of dialogue. First are arguments against pursuing, for example, wealth, followed by arguments in favor. Arguments against come first because this is the less conventional viewpoint, and therefore more intellectually challenging. The resulting debate between con and pro attitudes toward wealth, power, fame, praise, glory, and physical pleasure may be a good deal less artistic than Plato's *Dialogues*, which have something of the same purpose, but the plainer and simpler approach employed herein has the virtue of being straightforward and convenient. If readers will send us additional passages (with citations) they think should be included in these debates, debates about how each of us should order some of the essentials of our lives, we will be happy to consider them for future editions.

# WEALTH

## ARGUMENTS AGAINST THE PURSUIT OF WEALTH*

### BASIC ARGUMENTS

1. I cannot afford to waste my time making money.

> JEAN LOUIS RODOLPHE AGASSIZ ◆ 1807–1873
> Letter refusing lecture course offer

2. Better is bread with a happy heart
   Than wealth with vexation.

> AMENEMOPE ◆ C. 11TH CENTURY B.C.E.
> *The Instruction of Amenemope,* ch. 6

3. Where there is money, there is fighting.

> MARIAN ANDERSON ◆ 1902–1993
> Quoted in Kosti Vehanen, *Marian Anderson: A Portrait*

4. How can he get wisdom…whose talk is of bullocks?

> *Ecclesiasticus* 38:25 (Apocrypha)

---

* *Arguments for* … begin on page 32.

* *Arguments for* … begin on page 32.

1 ᔞ

5.  You canna expect to be baith grand and comfortable.

    J(AMES) M(ATTHEW) BARRIE ♦ 1860–1937
    *The Little Minister*

6.  Better is a handful with quietness, than both the hands full with travail and vexation of spirit.

    *Ecclesiastes* 4:6

7.  The sleep of a laboring man is sweet...but the abundance of the rich will not suffer him to sleep.

    *Ecclesiastes* 5:12

8.  All that a man hath will he give for his life.

    *Job* 2:4

9.  He heapeth up riches, and knoweth not who shall gather them.

    *Psalms* 39:6

10. *Daughter:* But Mama, wouldn't you like to be rich?
    *Mama:* I'd like to be rich as much as I'd like to be ten foot tall—good for some things, bad for others.

    DEWITT BODEEN ♦ 1908–1988
    From the 1948 film *I Remember Mama,* directed by George Stevens

11. Less is more.

    ROBERT BROWNING ♦ 1812–1889
    "Andrea Del Sarto," *Men and Women*

12. There is something to be said for losing one's possessions, after nothing can be done about it. I had loved my Nanking home and the little treasures it had contained, the lovely garden I had made, my life with friends and students. Well, that was over. I had nothing at all now except the old clothes I stood in. I should have felt sad, and I was quite shocked to realize that I did not feel sad at all. On the contrary, I had a lively sense of adventure merely at being alive and free, even of possessions. No one expected anything of me. I had no obligations, no duties, no tasks. I was nothing but a refugee, someone totally different from the busy young woman I had been.

PEARL S(YDENSTRICKER) BUCK ◆ 1892–1973
*My Several Worlds*

13. It is curious that money, which is the most valuable thing in life, excepis excipiendis, should be the most fatal corrupter of music, literature, painting and all the arts. As soon as any art is pursued with a view of money, then farewell, in ninety-nine cases out of a hundred, all hope of genuine good work.

SAMUEL BUTLER ◆ 1835–1902
*Note-Books* XI

14. There is a degree of poverty that has no disgrace belonging to it; that degree of it, I mean, in which a man enjoys clean linen and good company; and if I never sink below this degree of it, I care not if I never rise above it.

WILLIAM COWPER ◆ 1731–1800
Letter to Clotworthy Rowley, September 2, 1762

15. No wealth in the world can help humanity forward, even in the hands of the most devoted workers in this cause.... Can anyone imagine Moses, Jesus, or Gandhi armed with the money-bags of Carnegie?

> ALBERT EINSTEIN ◆ 1879–1955
> *Ideas and Opinions of Albert Einstein*

16. Money helps, though not so much as you think when you don't have it.

> LOUISE ERDRICH ◆ 1951–
> *The Bingo Palace Insulation*

17. Our life on earth is, and ought to be, material and carnal. But we have not yet learned to manage our materialism and carnality properly; they are still entangled with the desire for ownership.

> E(DWARD) M(ORGAN) FORSTER ◆ 1879–1970
> *Abinger Harvest My Wood*

18. Riches are gotten with pain, kept with care, and lost with grief.

> THOMAS FULLER ◆ 1654–1734
> *Gnomologia*

19. He is not fit for riches who is afraid to use them.

> Ibid., 1934

20. Rich men feel misfortunes that fly over poor men's heads.

> Ibid., 4035

21.  Riches rather enlarge than satisfy appetites.

*Ibid., 4048*

22.  I am indeed rich, since my income is superior to my expense, and my expense is equal to my wishes.

EDWARD GIBBON ◆ 1737–1794
*Autobiography*

23.  Thirst, hunger, and nakedness are positive evils: but wealth is relative; and a prince, who would be rich in a private station, may be exposed by the increase of his wants to all the anxiety and bitterness of poverty.

EDWARD GIBBON ◆ 1737–1794
*Decline and Fall of the Roman Empire* LXI

24.  A tragic irony of life is that we so often achieve success or financial independence after the chief reason for which we sought it has passed away.

ELLEN GLASGOW ◆ 1873–1945
*The Woman Within*

25.  The more flesh, the more worms.
     The more possessions, the more worry.

HILLEL ◆ FL. 30 B.C.E.–10
*The Living Talmud: The Wisdom of the Fathers
and Its Classical Commentaries*

26.  Wealth is friends, home, father, brother, title to respect and fame.

*Hitopadesa ("Book of Good Counsels"):
Fables and Proverbs from the Sanskrit* ◆ *c. 500*

27. It is neither wealth nor splendor, but tranquility and occupation, which give happiness.

> THOMAS JEFFERSON ♦ 1743–1826
> Letter to Mrs. A.S. Marks

28. You don't seem to realize that a poor person who is unhappy is in a better position than a rich person who is unhappy. Because the poor person has hope. He thinks money would help.

> JEAN KERR ♦ 1923–2003
> *Poor Richard*

29. People who are rich want to be richer, but what's the difference? You can't take it with you.

> MARTINA NAVRATILOVA ♦ 1956–
> *Martina*

30. An object in possession seldom retains the same charm that it had in pursuit.

> PLINY THE YOUNGER (GAIUS PLINIUS
> CAECILIUS SECUNDUS) ♦ C. 61–C. 112
> *Letters* 2.15.1

31. No one need go into alleys to hunt up wretchedness; they can find it in perfection among the rich and fashionable of every land and nation.

> ELIZA POTTER ♦ 1802–1888
> Introduction, *A Hairdresser's Experience in High Life*

32. Most people seek after what they do not possess and are thus enslaved by the very things they want to acquire.

> ANWAR AL-SADAT ♦ 1918–1981
> *In Search of Identity*

33. Money is that dear thing which, if you're not careful,
    you can squander your whole life thinking of.

    MARY JO SALTER ◆ 1954–
    *A Benediction* 6

34. The greatest evidence of demoralization is the respect
    paid to wealth.

    GEORGES SAND (AMANDINE AURORE LUCILE DUPIN) ◆ 1804–1876
    *French Wit and Wisdom*

35. If thou art rich, thou'rt poor;
    For, like an ass whose back with ingots bows,
    Thou bear'st thy heavy riches but a journey,
    And death unloads thee.

    WILLIAM SHAKESPEARE ◆ 1564–1616
    *Measure for Measure* III, i, 25

36. [W]hen thou art old and rich,
    Thou hast neither heat, affection, limb, nor beauty,
    To make thy riches pleasant.

    Ibid., III, i, 32

37. [T]hey are as sick that surfeit with too much as they
    that starve with nothing.

    WILLIAM SHAKESPEARE ◆ 1564–1616
    *The Merchant of Venice* I, ii, 5

38. [N]othing can we call our own but death
    And that small model of the barren earth
    Which serves as paste and cover to our bones.

    WILLIAM SHAKESPEARE ◆ 1564–1616
    *King Richard II,* III, ii, 152

39. Poor and content is rich and rich enough,
But riches fineless is as poor as winter
To him that ever fears he shall be poor.

> WILLIAM SHAKESPEARE ◆ 1564–1616
> *Othello* III, iii, 172

40. [S]aint-seducing gold.

> WILLIAM SHAKESPEARE ◆ 1564–1616
> *Romeo and Juliet* I, i, 220

41. It is the wretchedness of being rich that you have to live with rich people.

> LOGAN PEARSALL SMITH ◆ 1865–1946
> "In the World," *Afterthoughts*

42. I do want to get rich but I never want to do what there is to do to get rich.

> GERTRUDE STEIN ◆ 1874–1946
> *Everybody's Autobiography*

43. The price we have to pay for money is paid in liberty.

> ROBERT LOUIS STEVENSON ◆ 1850–1894
> *Familiar Studies of Men and Books*

44. Money is a new form of slavery....

> LEO NIKOLAEVICH TOLSTOY ◆ 1828–1910
> *What Are We to Do?*

45. The first half of life consists of the capacity to enjoy without the chance; the last half consists of the chance without the capacity.

> MARK TWAIN (SAMUEL LANGHORNE CLEMENS) ◆ 1835–1910
> Letter to Edward L. Dimmitt, July 19, 1901

46. He who possesses most must be most afraid of loss.

LEONARDO DA VINCI ◆ 1452–1519
*Notebooks*

47. What's wrong with it [our present-day society] is money, honey, money.

MARGARET WALKER ◆ 1915–1998
Quoted in Claudia Tate, *Black Women Writers at Work*

48. Money is only useful when you get rid of it. It is like the odd card in "Old Maid"; the player who is finally left with it has lost.

EVELYN WAUGH ◆ 1903–1966
"Kicking Against the Goad," *Commonweal* magazine, March 11, 1949

49. The difference between a little money and no money at all is enormous.... And the difference between a little money and an enormous amount of money is very slight....

THORNTON WILDER ◆ 1897–1975
*The Matchmaker*, Act 4

50. From the respect paid to property flow, as from a poisoned fountain, most of the evils and vices which render his world such a dreary scene to the contemplative mind.

MARY WOLLSTONECRAFT ◆ 1759–1797
*A Vindication of the Rights of Woman* IX

## PHILOSOPHICAL ARGUMENTS

51.  Receive wealth or prosperity without arrogance; and be ready to let it go.

MARCUS AURELIUS ANTONINUS ♦ 121–180
*Meditations* VII, 33

52.  So long as external things are sought or possessed only in a small quantity, and as much as is required for a mere livelihood, such care does not hinder one much, and consequently is not inconsistent with the perfection of Christian life.... Yet the possession of much wealth increases the weight of care, which is a great distraction to man's mind and hinders him from giving himself wholly to God's service.

THOMAS AQUINAS ♦ C. 1225–1274
*Summa Theologica*

53.  Happiness...must be some form of contemplation. But, being a man, one will also need external prosperity; for our nature is not self-sufficient for the purpose of contemplation, but our body also must be healthy and must have food and other attention. Still, we must not think that the man who is to be happy will need many things or great things...for self-sufficiency and action do not involve excess, and we can do noble acts without ruling earth and sea.

ARISTOTLE ♦ 384–322 B.C.E.
*Ethics*

54. Some persons are led to believe that . . . the whole idea of their lives is that they ought either to increase their money without limit, or at any rate not to lose it. The origin of this disposition in men is that they are intent upon living only, and not upon living well; and, as their desires are unlimited, they also desire that the means of gratifying them should be without limit.

ARISTOTLE ♦ 384–322 B.C.E.
*Politics*

55. The people who believe most that our greatness and welfare are proved by our being very rich, and who most give their lives and thoughts to becoming rich, are just the very people whom we call Philistines.

MATTHEW ARNOLD ♦ 1822–1888
*Culture and Anarchy*

56. Let us suppose a case of two men. . . . Of these two men let us suppose that one is poor, or rather of middling circumstances; the other very rich. But the rich man is anxious with fears, pining with discontent, burning with covetousness, never secure, always uneasy, panting from the perpetual strife of his enemies, adding to his patrimony indeed by these miseries to an immense degree, and by these additions also heaping up most bitter cares. But that other man of moderate wealth is contented with a small and compact estate, most dear to his own family, enjoying the sweetest peace with his kindred neighbours and friends, in piety religious, benignant in mind, healthy in body, in life frugal, in manners chaste, in conscience secure. I know

11 ﻉﻭ

not whether anyone can be such a fool, that he dare hesitate which to prefer.

SAINT AUGUSTINE ◆ 354–430
*City of God* IV, 3

57.  It is not earthly riches which make us or our sons happy; for they must either be lost by us in our lifetime, or be possessed when we are dead, by whom we know not, or perhaps by whom we would not.

Ibid., V, 18

58.  Of great riches there is no real use, except in the distribution; the rest is but conceit.

FRANCIS BACON ◆ 1561–1626
*Essays on Riches*

59.  I understand that only the rich can be members of Dr. C_____'s church. The Lord Christ, also, is therefore ineligible. I will remain outside with Him.

AMELIA E. BARR ◆ 1831–1919
*All the Days of My Life*

60.  What in fact is it that you are looking for in all this outcry against Fortune? To put poverty to flight with plenty? If so, it has turned out the very opposite. The more varied your precious possessions, the more help you need to protect them, and the old saying is proved correct, he who hath much, wants much. And the contrary is true as well, he needs least who measures wealth according to the needs of nature, and not the excesses of ostentation.

(ANICUS MANLIUS SEVERINUS) BOETHIUS ◆ C. 480–524
*The Consolation of Philosophy* II, V

61. It seems as if you feel a lack of any blessing of your own inside you, which is driving you to seek your blessings in things separate and external. And so when a being endowed with a godlike quality in virtue of his rational nature thinks that his only splendour lies in the possession of inanimate goods, it is the overthrow of the natural order. Other creatures are content with what is their own, but you, whose mind is made in the image of God, seek to adorn your superior nature with inferior objects, oblivious of the great wrong you do your Creator.

Ibid.

62. My contention is that no good thing harms its owner, a thing which you won't gainsay. But wealth very often does harm its owners, for all the most criminal elements of the population who are thereby all the more covetous of other people's property are convinced that they alone are worthy to possess all the gold and precious stones there are.

Ibid.

63. How splendid, then, the blessing of mortal riches is! Once won, they never leave you carefree again.

Ibid.

64. "You earthly creatures, you also dream of your origin, however faint the vision. You do have some sort of notion, unclear as it is, of the true goal of happiness, and so an instinctive sense of direction actually guides you towards the true good, only various errors lead you astray. Consider, therefore, whether men really

can reach their appointed goal by the means with which they think they are going to win happiness. If money or position or the rest do bring some sort of condition which doesn't seem to lack any of the good things, I will join you in admitting that some people do become happy through the possession of them. But if money and the rest can't achieve what they promise and are actually lacking in the greater number of good things, it will be quite obvious that in them men are snatching at a false appearance of happiness.

"So first I will ask you a few questions, since you yourself were a wealthy man not long ago. In the midst of all that great store of wealth, was your mind never troubled by worry arising from a feeling of injury?"

"Yes it was," I replied; "in fact I can't remember when my mind was ever free from some sort of worry!"

"And that was either because something was missing which you didn't want to be missing, or because something was present which you would have preferred not to have been present."

"Yes!"

"You wanted the presence of one thing and the absence of another?"

"Yes."

"Now a man must be lacking something if he misses it, mustn't he?"

"Yes."

"And if a man lacks something he is not in every way self sufficient?"

"No."

"And so you felt this insufficiency even though you were supplied with wealth?"

"Yes, I did."

"So that wealth cannot make a man free of want and self-sufficient—though this was the very promise we saw it offering. And this, too, I think, is a point of great importance, namely the fact that money has no inherent property such as to stop it being taken away from those who possess it, against their will."

I had to agree.

"You can hardly do otherwise," she continued, "when it can happen that someone takes it from another against his will because he is stronger. What else are the lawsuits for except to recover moneys that have been stolen by fraud or violence?"

"That is true!"

"So that a man will need outside help to protect his money."

"Yes."

"But he won't need it if he doesn't possess any money which may be lost?"

"No."

"So the situation has been reversed. Wealth which was thought to make a man self-sufficient in fact makes him dependent on outside help. In which case, what is the way in which riches remove want? If you say that rich people do have the means of satisfying hunger and driving away thirst and cold, I will reply that although want can be checked in this way by riches, it can't be entirely removed. Every hungry and clamorous want may be satisfied with the help of riches, but the want which admits of being satisfied necessarily still remains. There is no need for me to mention that nature is satisfied with little, whereas nothing satisfies greed. So that, if so far from being able to remove want, riches create a want of their own, there is no reason for you to believe that they confer self-sufficiency."

Ibid., III, III

65. "Here shall I dwell in the season of rains, and here in winter and summer"; thus thinks the fool, but he does not think of death. For death carries away the man whose mind is self-satisfied with his children and his flocks, even as a torrent carries away a sleeping village.

BUDDHA (SIDDHARTHA GAUTAMA) ◆ C. 563–483 B.C.E.
*The Dhammapada* 20.76

66. "These are my sons. This is my wealth." In this way the fool troubles himself. He is not even the owner of himself: how much less of his sons and of his wealth!

Ibid.

67. The wise do not call a strong fetter that which is made of iron, of wood or of rope; much stronger is the fetter of passion for gold and for jewels, for sons or for wives.

Ibid.

68. Wealth *per se* I never too much valued, and my acquaintance with its possessors has by no means increased my veneration for it.

FRANCES BURNEY ◆ 1752–1840
*Diary,* December 8, 1782

69. With coarse rice to eat, with water to drink, and my bended arm for a pillow—I have still joy in the midst of these things. Riches and honors acquired by unrighteousness are to me as a floating cloud.

> CONFUCIUS ◆ 551–479 B.C.E.
> *Analects* 7:15

70. Love of money is the mother of all evils.

> DIOGENES THE CYNIC ◆ C. 400–325 B.C.E.
> In Diogenes Laertius, *Lives of Eminent Philosophers*

71. Our expense is almost all for conformity. It is for cake that we all run in debt.

> RALPH WALDO EMERSON ◆ 1803–1882
> *Journals*

72. These arguments do not follow: "I am richer than you, therefore I am superior to you"; "I am more eloquent than you, therefore I am superior to you." No, these are the arguments that follow: "I am richer than you, therefore my property is superior to yours"; "I am more eloquent than you, therefore my style is superior to yours." But you, after all, are neither property nor style.

> EPICTETUS ◆ C. 55–135
> *The Handbook of Epictetus* 44

73. In things relating to the body take just so much as bare need requires, that is to say, in things such as meat, drink, clothing, housing, and household slaves. But cut out everything that is for show and luxury.

> Ibid., 33

74. I am thrilled with pleasure in the body, when I live on bread and water, and I spit upon luxurious pleasures not for their own sake, but because of the inconveniences that follow them.

EPICURUS ◆ 341–270 B.C.E.
*Fragments* 37

75. Many men when they have acquired riches have not found the escape from their ills but only a change to greater ills.

Ibid., 72

76. Nature's wealth at once had its bounds and is easy to procure; but the wealth of vain fancies recedes to an infinite distance.

EPICURUS ◆ 341–270 B.C.E.
*The Principal Doctrines* 15

77. Unlimited wealth is great poverty.

EPICURUS ◆ 341–270 B.C.E.
*Vatican Sayings* 25

78. Some men throughout their lives gather together the means of life, for they do not see that the draught swallowed by all of us at birth is a draught of death.

Ibid., 30

79. A free life cannot acquire many possessions, because this is not easy to do without servility to mobs or monarchs, yet it possesses all things in unfailing abundance; and if by chance it obtains many pos-

sessions, it is easy to distribute them so as to win the gratitude of neighbours.

*Ibid.*, 57

80. Nothing is sufficient for him to whom what is sufficient seems little.

*Ibid.*, 68

81. The praises of poverty need once more to be boldly sung. We have grown literally afraid to be poor. We despise anyone who elects to be poor in order to simplify and save his inner life. If he does not join the general scramble and pant with the moneymaking street, we deem him spiritless and lacking in ambition. We have lost the power even of imagining what the ancient idealization of poverty could have meant: the liberation from material attachments, the unbribed soul, the manlier indifference, the paying our way by what we are or do and not by what we have, the right to fling away our life at any moment irresponsibly—the more athletic trim, in short, the moral fighting shape.

WILLIAM JAMES ◆ 1842–1910
*The Varieties of Religious Experience*

82. He hath filled the hungry with good things; and the rich he hath sent empty away.

JESUS ◆ C. 4 B.C.E.–30
*Luke* 1:53

83. But woe unto you that are rich! for ye have received your consolation.

*Ibid.*, 6:24

84. Take heed, and beware of covetousness: for a man's life consisteth not in the abundance of the things which he possesseth. The ground of a certain rich man brought forth plentifully: And he thought within himself, saying, What shall I do, because I have no room where to bestow my fruits? And he said, This will I do: I will pull down my barns, and build greater; and there will I bestow all my fruits and my goods. And I will say to my soul, Soul, thou hast much goods laid up for many years; take thine ease, eat, drink, and be merry. But God said unto him, Thou fool, this night thy soul shall be required of thee: then whose shall those things be, which thou hast provided? So is he that layeth up treasure for himself, and is not rich toward God.

Ibid., 12:15-21

85. For where your treasure is, there will your heart be also.

JESUS ◆ C. 4 B.C.E.–30
*Matthew* 6:21

86. No man can serve two masters: for either he will hate the one, and love the other; or else he will hold to the one, and despise the other. Ye cannot serve God and mammon.

Ibid., 6:24

87. Therefore I say unto you, Take no thought for your life, what ye shall eat, or what ye shall drink; nor yet for your body, what ye shall put on. Is not the life more than meat, and the body than raiment? Behold

the fowls of the air: for they sow not, neither do they reap, nor gather into barns; yet your heavenly Father feedeth them. Are ye not much better than they? Which of you by taking thought can add one cubit unto his stature? And why take ye thought for raiment? Consider the lilies of the field, how they grow; they toil not, neither do they spin: And yet I say unto you, That even Solomon in all his glory was not arrayed like one of these. Wherefore, if God so clothe the grass of the field, which to day is, and to morrow is cast into the oven, shall he not much more clothe you, O ye of little faith? Therefore take no thought, saying, What shall we eat? or, What shall we drink? or, Wherewithal shall we be clothed? (For after all these things do the Gentiles seek:) for your heavenly Father knoweth that ye have need of all these things.

Ibid., 6:25-33

88. Lay not up for yourselves treasures upon earth, where moth and rust doth corrupt, and where thieves break through and steal.

Ibid., 11:19

89. The care of this world, and the deceitfulness of riches.

Ibid., 13:22

90. If thou wilt be perfect, go and sell that thou hast, and give to the poor, and thou shalt have treasure in heaven: and come and follow me. Verily I say unto you, That a rich man shall hardly enter into the kingdom of heaven. And again I say unto you, It is

easier for a camel to go through the eye of a needle, than for a rich man to enter into the kingdom of God. With men this is impossible; but with God all things are possible.

*Ibid., 19:21-26*

91.  When the Son of man shall come in his glory, and all the holy angels with him, then shall he sit upon the throne of his glory: And before him shall be gathered all nations: and he shall separate them one from another, as a shepherd divideth his sheep from the goats: And he shall set the sheep on his right hand, but the goats on the left. Then shall the King say unto them on his right hand, Come, ye blessed of my Father, inherit the kingdom prepared for you from the foundation of the world: For I was an hungred, and ye gave me meat: I was thirsty, and ye gave me drink: I was a stranger, and ye took me in: Naked, and ye clothed me: I was sick, and ye visited me: I was in prison, and ye came unto me. Then shall the righteous answer him, saying, Lord, when saw we thee an hungred, and fed thee? or thirsty, and gave thee drink? When saw we thee a stranger, and took thee in? or naked, and clothed thee? Or when saw we thee sick, or in prison, and came unto thee? And the King shall answer and say unto them, Verily I say unto you, Inasmuch as ye have done it unto one of the least of these my brethren, ye have done it unto me. Then shall he say also unto them on the left hand, Depart from me, ye cursed, into everlasting fire, prepared for the devil and his angels: For I was an hungred, and ye gave me no meat: I was thirsty, and ye gave me no drink:

I was a stranger, and ye took me not in: naked, and ye clothed me not: sick, and in prison, and ye visited me not. Then shall they also answer him, saying, Lord, when saw we thee an hungred, or athirst, or a stranger, or naked, or sick, or in prison, and did not minister unto thee? Then shall he answer them, saying, Verily I say unto you, Inasmuch as ye did it not to one of the least of these, ye did it not to me. And these shall go away into everlasting punishment: but the righteous into life eternal.

*Ibid.*, 25:31-46

92. Jesus went into the temple...overthrew the tables of the money changers, and the seats of them that sold doves.

*Mark* 11:15

93. Your worldly riches are transitory, but God's reward is everlasting.

*The Qur'an (Koran)*

94. And Noah said: "Lord, my people disobey me, and follow those whose wealth and offspring will only hasten their perdition."

Ibid.

95. The sage does not accumulate for himself. The more he uses for others, the more he has himself. The more he gives to others, the more he possesses of his own.

LAO-TZU ◆ C. 604–C. 531 B.C.E.
*The Way of Lao-tzu* 81

96. Riches do not bring freedom from sorrow and are of no avail for eternal happiness, but rather are obstacles.

POPE LEO XIII ◆ 1810–1903
*Rerum novarum,* May 15, 1891

97. The greatest wealth is to live content with little, for there is never want where the mind is satisfied.

LUCRETIUS (TITUS LUCRETIUS) ◆ 99–55 B.C.E.
*On the Nature of Things* V

98. Then, too, want of food would give over their drooping limbs to death. But in contrast now it is surfeit of good things that brings them low.

Ibid., V, 999

99. The matter, form, effect, and goal of riches are worthless. That's why our Lord God generally gives riches to crude asses to whom he doesn't give anything else.

MARTIN LUTHER ◆ 1483–1546
*Table Talk* CLXVII

100. Where great wealth is, there are also all manner of sins; for through wealth comes pride, through pride, dissension, through dissension, wars, through wars, poverty, through poverty, great distress and misery. Therefore, they that are rich, must yield a strict and great account; for to whom much is given, of him much will be required.

Ibid., CLXV

101. Wealth is the smallest thing on earth, the least gift that God has bestowed on mankind.

*Ibid.*, CLXVII

102. He who wishes to be benevolent will not be rich.

MENCIUS ◆ 372–289 B.C.E.
*Works* III, i

103. I want death to find me planting my cabbages.

MICHEL EYQUEM DE MONTAIGNE ◆ 1533–1592
*Essays* I

104. As having nothing, and yet possessing all things.

SAINT PAUL ◆ 1ST CENTURY
*2 Corinthians* 6:10

105. For the love of money is the root of all evil: which while some coveted after, they have erred from the faith, and pierced themselves through with many sorrows.

SAINT PAUL ◆ 1ST CENTURY
*1 Timothy* 6:10

106. We brought nothing into this world, and it is certain we can carry nothing out.

*Ibid.*, 6:7

107. [T]he makers of fortunes have a second love of money as a creation of their own, resembling the affection of authors for their own poems, or of parents for their children, besides that natural love of it for the sake

of use and profit which is common to them and all
men. And hence they are very bad company, for they
can talk about nothing but the praises of wealth.

PLATO ◆ C. 428–348 B.C.E.
*The Republic* I

108. But let him know how to choose the mean and avoid
extremes on either side, as far as possible, not only
in this life but in all that which is to come. For this
is the way of happiness.

Ibid., X

109. Money has never appeared to me as valuable as it
is generally considered. More than that, it has never
even appeared to me particularly convenient. It is
good for nothing in itself; it has to be changed before
it can be enjoyed; one is obliged to buy, to bargain, to
be often cheated, to pay dearly, to be badly served.
I should like something which is good in quality;
with my money I am sure to get it bad.

JEAN JACQUES ROUSSEAU ◆ 1712–1778
*Confessions* I

110. It is one of the misfortunes of the rich to be cheated
on all sides; what wonder they think ill of mankind!
It is riches that corrupt men, and the rich are rightly
the first to feel the defects of the only tool they know.
Everything is ill-done for them, except what they do
themselves, and they do next to nothing.

JEAN JACQUES ROUSSEAU ◆ 1712–1778
*Emile* I

111. It is physically impossible for a well-educated, intellectual, or brave man to make money the chief object of his thoughts; as physically impossible as it is for him to make his dinner the principal object of them.

JOHN RUSKIN ◆ 1819–1900
*The Crown of Wild Olive*

112. I desire... to leave this one great fact clearly stated. THERE IS NO WEALTH BUT LIFE.

JOHN RUSKIN ◆ 1819–1900
*Ethics of the Dust*

113. Riches are intended for the comfort of life, and not life for the purpose of hoarding riches.

SA'DI ◆ C. 1184–1291
*Gulistan* 8.I

114. It is difficult, if not impossible, to define the limits which reason should impose on the desire for wealth; for there is no absolute or definite amount of wealth which will satisfy a man. The amount is always relative.... A man never feels the loss of things which it never occurs to him to ask for; he is just as happy without them; whilst another, who may have a hundred times as much, feels miserable because he has not got the one thing he wants. In fact, here too, every man has an horizon of his own, and he will expect as much as he thinks it is possible for him to get.

ARTHUR SCHOPENHAUER ◆ 1788–1860
"Property, or What a Man Has,"
*The Wisdom of Life and Counsels and Maxims*

115. It is not the man who has too little who is poor, but the one who hankers after more. What difference does it make how much there is laid away in a man's safe or in his barns, how many head of stock he grazes or how much capital he puts out at interest, if he is always after what is another's and only counts what he has yet to get, never what he has already. You ask what is the proper limit to a person's wealth? First, having what is essential, and second, having what is enough.

LUCIUS ANNAEUS SENECA ◆ C. 4 B.C.E.–54
*Letters to Lucilius* 2

116. What nature requires is obtainable, and within easy reach. It's for the superfluous we sweat.

Ibid., 4

117. Imagine that you've piled up all that a veritable host of rich men ever possessed, that fortune has carried you far beyond the bounds of wealth so far as any private individual is concerned, building you a roof of gold and clothing you in royal purple, conducting you to such a height of opulence and luxury that you hide the earth with marble floors—putting you in a position not merely to own, but to walk all over treasures—throw in sculptures, paintings, all that has been produced at tremendous pains by all the arts to satisfy extravagance: all these things will only induce to you a craving for even bigger things. Natural desires are limited; those which spring from false opinions have nowhere to stop, for falsity has no point of termination.

Ibid., 16

118. Many a man has found the acquisition of wealth only a change, not an end of miseries.

Ibid., 17

119. A great fortune is a great slavery.

LUCIUS ANNAEUS SENECA ◆ C. 4 B.C.E.–54
"To Polybius on Consolation," *Moral Essays* 6, 5

120. Acquisitiveness also narrows interests and limits appreciation. The number of things that we can possess is only a small fraction of those that we can enjoy without owning them. To admire without coveting greatly increases contentment. Instead of desiring the beautiful things that we see, we should be grateful that they exist for our enjoyment without our laborious care. This is eminently true of all the grand and lovely sights that nature presents to us and, even, of many of our friends' and neighbors' possessions—their gardens, the façades of their houses, the pictures on their walls.

ALEXANDER FRANK SKUTCH ◆ 1904–2004
*Life Ascending*

121. With the greater part of rich people, the chief enjoyment of riches consists in the parade of riches, which in their eyes is never so complete as when they appear to possess those decisive marks of opulence which nobody can possess but themselves.

ADAM SMITH ◆ 1723–1790
*The Wealth of Nations* I, 11

122. [The rich person] is at all times surrounded by un-known enemies, whom, though he never provoked, he can never appease.

Ibid., V, 1

123. I do nothing but go about persuading all, old and young alike, not to take thought for your persons or your properties, but first chiefly to care about the greatest improvement of the soul.

SOCRATES ◆ C. 428–348 B.C.E.<br>Quoted in Plato, Apology

124. If [Jacobinism] were right in declaring that man is born to be happy, he would not be born to die. Since his body is doomed to die, his task on earth evidently must be of a more spiritual nature. It cannot be un-restrained enjoyment of everyday life. It cannot be the search for the best ways to obtain material goods and then cheerfully get the most out of them. It has to be the fulfillment of a permanent, earnest duty so that one's life journey may become an experience of moral growth, in that one may leave life a better human being than one started it.

ALEXANDER SOLZHENITSYN ◆ 1918–<br>Address at Harvard University commencement

125. Those…who know the true use of money, and regulate the measure of wealth according to their needs, live contented with few things.

BARUCH SPINOZA ◆ 1632–1677<br>Ethics IV, Appendix XXIX

126. Nothing that is God's is obtainable by money.

TERTULLIAN (QUINTUS SEPTIMIUS) ◆ C. 160–240
*The Christian's Defence*

127. No man takes with him to Hades all his exceeding wealth.

THEOGNIS ◆ C. 545 B.C.E.
*Elegies* 1, 725

128. Most of the luxuries, and many of the so-called comforts of life, are not only not indispensable, but positive hindrances to the elevation of mankind. With respect to luxuries and comforts, the wisest have ever lived a more simple and meagre life than the poor. The ancient philosophers, Chinese, Hindoo, Persian, and Greek, were a class than which none has been poorer in outward riches, none so rich in inward. We know not much about them. It is remarkable that we know so much of them as we do. The same is true of the more modern reformers and benefactors of their race. None can be an impartial or wise observer of human life but from the vantage ground of what we should call voluntary poverty. Of a life of luxury the fruit is luxury, whether in agriculture, or commerce, or literature, or art. There are nowadays professors of philosophy, but not philosophers.

HENRY DAVID THOREAU ◆ 1817–1862
*Walden*

129. Simplicity, simplicity, simplicity! I say, let your affairs be as two or three, and not a hundred or a thousand; instead of a million count half a dozen, and keep your accounts on your thumb-nail.

Ibid.

# ARGUMENTS FOR
# THE PURSUIT OF WEALTH

## BASIC ARGUMENTS

130. The possession of gold has ruined fewer men than the lack of it. What noble enterprises have been checked and what fine souls have been blighted in the gloom of poverty the world will never know.

THOMAS BAILEY ALDRICH ◆ 1836–1907
*Ponkapog Papers*

131. A large income is the best recipe for happiness I ever heard of. It certainly may secure all the myrtle and turkey part of it.

JANE AUSTEN ◆ 1775–1817
*Mansfield Park*

132. It is a truth universally acknowledged, that a single man in possession of a good fortune, must be in want of a wife.

JANE AUSTEN ◆ 1775–1817
*Pride and Prejudice*

133. Money speaks sense in a language all nations understand.

APHRA BEHN ◆ 1640–1689
*The Rover* II, III, i

134. I'm tired of Love:
   I'm still more tired of Rhyme.
   But Money gives me pleasure all the time.

HILAIRE BELLOC ◆ 1870–1953
*Fatigue*

135. When I was running about this town a very poor fellow, I was a great arguer for the advantages of poverty; but I was, at the same time, very sorry to be poor....All the arguments which are brought to represent poverty as no evil, shew it to be evidently a great evil. You never find people labouring to convince you that you may live very happily upon a plentiful fortune.

JAMES BOSWELL ◆ 1740–1795
*Life of Johnson*

136. For hym was levere have at his beddes heed
Twenty bookes, clad in blak or reed,
Of Aristotle and his philosophie,
Than robes riche, or fithele, or gay sautrie,
But al be that he was a philosophre,
Yet hadde he but litel gold in cofre.

GEOFFREY CHAUCER ◆ 1343–1400
Prologue, *The Canterbury Tales* 1, 293

137. There are many to whom money has no personal appeal, but who can be tempted by the power it confers.

AGATHA CHRISTIE ◆ 1891–1976
*Crooked House*

138. Those who never think of money need a great deal of it.

AGATHA CHRISTIE ◆ 1891–1976
"The Second Gong," *Witness for the Prosecution*

139. Property is desirable as the ground work of moral independence, as a means of improving the faculties,

and of doing good to others, and as the agent in all that distinguishes the civilized man from the savage.

JAMES FENIMORE COOPER ◆ 1789–1851
*The American Democrat* XXVIII

140. I do not claim that all women, or a large portion of them, should enter into independent business relations with the world, but I do claim that all women should cultivate and respect in themselves an ability to make money.

ELLEN DEMAREST ◆ 1824–1898
Quoted in Anne L. MacDonald, *Feminine Ingenuity*

141. Money is coined liberty, and so it is ten times dearer to a man who is deprived of freedom. If money is jingling in his pocket, he is half consoled, even though he cannot spend it.

FYODOR MIKHAILOVICH DOSTOEVSKY ◆ 1821–1881
*The House of the Dead* 1.1

142. Well! some people talk of morality, and some of religion, but give me a little snug property.

MARIA EDGEWORTH ◆ 1767–1849
*The Absentee*

143. Money's the wise man's religion, little man. The rest is mere bluff and purple patches.

EURIPIDES ◆ 485–406 B.C.E.
*Cyclops* 316

144. [T]he most important thing on earth to men today is money.

JANET (GENET) FLANNER ◆ 1892–1978
*Paris Journal*

145. In my book, anyone pretending he has no interest in money is either a fool or a knave.

LESLIE FORD ◆ 1898–1983
*Invitation to Murder*

146. Wealth is not without its advantages and the case to the contrary, although it has often been made, has never proved widely persuasive.

JOHN KENNETH GALBRAITH ◆ 1908–
*The Affluent Society*

147. Money…ranks with love as man's greatest joy…[although] it ranks with death as his greatest source of anxiety.

JOHN KENNETH GALBRAITH ◆ 1908–
*The Age of Uncertainty*

148. To have money is to be virtuous, honest, beautiful and witty. And to be without is to be ugly and boring and stupid and useless.

JEAN GIRAUDOUX ◆ 1882–1944
*The Madwoman of Chaillot*

149. Time is money—says the vulgarest saw known to any age or people. Turn it round about, and you get a precious truth—Money is time.

GEORGE (ROBERT) GISSING ◆ 1857–1903
*The Private Papers of Henry Ryecroft*

150. The advantage of riches is that they enable a man to indulge his passions, and help him to bear up against whatever harm befalls him.

HERODOTUS ◆ C. 485–C. 425 B.C.E.
*Histories* I

151. Give us the luxuries of life, and we will dispense with its necessaries.

OLIVER WENDELL HOLMES ♦ 1809–1894
*The Autocrat of the Breakfast-Table* VI

152. Money creates taste.

JENNY HOLZER ♦ 1950–
*Truisms*

153. The men of greatest usefulness are those who have a surplus; those who have only good will and love for their fellows cannot equal in well-doing those who have money and success to their credit.

E(DGAR) W(ATSON) HOWE ♦ 1853–1937
*The Blessing of Business*

154. There are few ways in which a man can be more innocently employed than in getting money.

SAMUEL JOHNSON ♦ 1709–1784
Quoted in Boswell, *Life of Johnson,* March 27, 1775

155. Go into the street, and give one man a lecture on morality, and another a shilling, and see which will respect you most.

Ibid., July 20, 1763

156. No man but a blockhead ever wrote, except for money.

Ibid., April 5, 1776

157. Your economy, I suppose, begins now to be settled; your expenses are adjusted to your revenue, and

all your people in their proper places. Resolve not to be poor: whatever you have, spend less. Poverty is a great enemy to human happiness; it certainly destroys liberty, and it makes some virtues impracticable, and others extremely difficult.

Ibid., December 7, 1782

158. Get money; still get money, boy, no matter by what means.

BEN JONSON ♦ C. 1573–1637
*Every Man in His Humour* II, iii

159. Affected simplicity is an elegant imposture.

FRANÇOIS, DUC DE LA ROCHEFOUCAULD ♦ 1613–1680
*Maxims*

160. O money, money, how blindly thou hast been worshipped, and how stupidly abused! Thou art health, and liberty, and strength; and he that has thee may rattle his pockets at the foul fiend.

CHARLES LAMB ♦ 1775–1834
Letter to Coleridge, June 7, 1809

161. Having money is just the best thing in the world.

MADONNA (CICCONE) ♦ 1958
Quoted in David Ansen, "Magnificent Maverick,"
*Cosmopolitan* magazine, May 1990, p. 311

162. I must say I hate money but it's the lack of it I hate most.

KATHERINE MANSFIELD ♦ 1888–1923
Quoted in Antony Alpers, *Katherine Mansfield*

163. The value of money is that with it you can tell anyone to go to the devil.

> W(ILLIAM) SOMERSET MAUGHAM ♦ 1874–1965
> (Attributed)

164. The urbane activity with which a man receives money is really marvellous, considering that we so earnestly believe money to be the root of all earthly ills, and that on no account can a monied man enter heaven. Ah! How cheerfully we consign ourselves to perdition!

> HERMAN MELVILLE ♦ 1819–1891
> *Moby-Dick*

165. Get wealth when you have it not; guard what you have got; increase what you have guarded; and bestow on worthy persons what you have increased.

> PANCHATANTRA ♦ C. 5TH CENTURY
> I

166. Wealth to us is not mere material for vainglory but an opportunity for achievement....

> PERICLES ♦ C. 495–429 B.C.E.
> Quoted in Thucydides, *The History of the Peloponnesian War* II
> (Funeral Oration of Pericles)

167. I bless God I do find that I am worth more than ever I yet was, which is £6,200, for which the Holy Name of God be praised!

> SAMUEL PEPYS ♦ 1633–1703
> *Diary,* October 31, 1666

168. But it is pretty to see what money will do.

> Ibid., March 21, 1667

169. He that has a penny in his purse, is worth a penny:
Have and you shall be esteemed.

GAIUS PETRONIUS (PETRONIUS ARBITER) ◆ C. 27–66
*Satyricon*

170. I should like to live like a poor man, with a great
deal of money.

PABLO PICASSO ◆ 1881–1973
Quoted in Janet Flanner, *Janet Flanner's World*

171. Money is the barometer of a society's virtue.

AYN RAND ◆ 1905–1982
*Atlas Shrugged*

172. The American Dream is really money.

JILL ROBINSON ◆ 1936–
Quoted in Studs Terkel, *American Dreams* 1

173. The good Lord gave me my money.

JOHN D. ROCKEFELLER ◆ 1839–1937
Address to first graduating class, University of Chicago

174. A fool and her money are soon courted.

HELEN ROWLAND ◆ 1875–1950
*A Guide to Men*

175. Bell, book, and candle shall not drive me back,
When gold and silver becks me to come on.

WILLIAM SHAKESPEARE ◆ 1564–1616
*King John* III, iii, 12

176. More and more I am certain that the only difference
between man and animals is that men can count

and animals cannot and if they count they mostly do count money.

GERTRUDE STEIN ◆ 1874–1946
*Everybody's Autobiography*

177. No one would remember the Good Samaritan if he'd only had good intentions. He had money as well.

MARGARET THATCHER ◆ 1925–
Quoted in the London *Times,* January 12, 1986

178. I've been rich and I've been poor. Believe me, honey, rich is better.

SOPHIE TUCKER ◆ 1884–1966
*Some of These Days*

179. Some men worship rank, some worship heroes, some worship power, some worship God, and over these ideals they dispute—but they all worship money.

MARK TWAIN (SAMUEL LANGHORNE CLEMENS) ◆ 1835–1910
*Notebook*

180. The only way not to think about money is to have a great deal of it.

EDITH WHARTON ◆ 1862–1937
*The House of Mirth*

181. Indeed, I thought, slipping the silver into my purse, it is remarkable, remembering the bitterness of those days, what a change of temper a fixed income will bring about.

VIRGINIA WOOLF ◆ 1882–1941
*A Room of One's Own*

## PHILOSOPHICAL ARGUMENTS

182. Happiness may be defined as good fortune joined to virtue, or as independence, or as a life that is both agreeable and secure, or as plenty of property and slaves, with the capacity to get more.

> ARISTOTLE ◆ 384–322 B.C.E.
> *Rhetoric* I

183. Believe not much them that seem to despise riches....

> FRANCIS BACON ◆ 1561–1626
> *Of Riches*

184. The pulpit and the press have many commonplaces denouncing the thirst for wealth; but if men should take these moralists at their word and leave off aiming to be rich, the moralists would rush to rekindle at all hazards this love of power in the people, lest civilization should be undone.

> RALPH WALDO EMERSON ◆ 1803–1882
> "Wealth," *The Conduct of Life*

185. Wealth is well known to be a great comforter.

> PLATO ◆ C. 428–348 B.C.E.
> *The Republic* I

186. The friends of humanity cannot but wish that in all countries the laboring classes should have a taste for comforts and enjoyments, and that they should be stimulated by all legal means in their exertions

to procure them. There cannot be a better security against a superabundant population.

DAVID RICARDO ◆ 1771–1823
*Principles of Political Economy*

187. Everything else can satisfy only one wish, one need....Money alone is absolutely good, because it is not only a concrete satisfaction of one need in particular; it is an abstract satisfaction of all.

ARTHUR SCHOPENHAUER ◆ 1788–1860
"Property, or What a Man Has,"
*The Wisdom of Life and Counsels and Maxims*

188. People have declaimed against luxury for 2000 years, in verse and in prose, and people have always delighted in it.

VOLTAIRE (FRANÇOIS MARIE AROUET) ◆ 1694–1778
*Philosophical Dictionary*

# POWER

## ARGUMENTS AGAINST THE PURSUIT OF POWER*

---

### BASIC ARGUMENTS

---

1. Power tends to corrupt and absolute power corrupts absolutely.

   > LORD ACTON (JOHN E.E. DALBERG–ACTON) ◆ 1834–1902
   > Letter to Bishop Mandell Creighton, April 3, 1887

2. True happiness is of a retired nature, and an enemy to pomp and noise.

   > JOSEPH ADDISON ◆ 1672–1719
   > Quoted in *The Spectator*, March 17, 1711

3. "Must power always be for destruction?" said Anna. "That has so far been largely the experience."

   > SYBILLE VON SCHOENEBECK BEDFORD ◆ 1911–
   > *A Favorite of the Gods*

---

* *Arguments* <u>*for*</u> ... begin on page 63.

4. The highest branch is not the safest roost.

HENRY GEORGE BOHN ◆ 1796–1884
*Handbook of Proverbs*

5. If you are as happy, my dear sir, on entering this house as I am in leaving it and returning home, you are the happiest man in this country.

JAMES BUCHANAN ◆ 1791–1868
To Abraham Lincoln at the White House, March 4, 1861

6. What millions died—that Caesar might be great!

THOMAS CAMPBELL ◆ 1777–1844
*The Pleasures of Hope*

7. To be a great autocrat you must be a great barbarian.

JOSEPH CONRAD ◆ 1857–1924
*The Mirror of the Sea*

8. Omnipotence is bought with ceaseless fear.

PIERRE CORNEILLE ◆ 1606–1684
*Cinna* 4.1

9. The race is not to the swift, nor the battle to the strong.

*Ecclesiastes* 9:11

10. He that is today a king tomorrow shall die.

*Ecclesiasticus* 10:10 (Apocrypha)

11. Greatness consists in power, pride, insolence, and doing mischief to mankind....A great man and a great rogue are synonymous.

HENRY FIELDING ◆ 1707–1754
*Jonathan Wild*

12. Think, in this batter'd Caravanserai
    Whose Doorways are alternate Night and Day,
    How Sultan after Sultan with his Pomp
    Abode his Hour or two, and went his way.

    EDWARD FITZGERALD ◆ 1809–1883
    *The Rubáiyát of Omar Khayyam*

13. There is no more contemptible poison than power
    over one's fellow men.

    MAXIM GORKY (ALEKSEI PESHKOV) ◆ 1868–1936
    "Untimely Thoughts," in *Novaya Zhizn (New Life)*

14. Seest thou how God with his lightning smites always
    the bigger animals, and will not suffer them to wax
    insolent, while those of a lesser bulk chafe him not?
    How likewise his bolts fall ever on the highest houses
    and the tallest trees? So plainly does He love to bring
    down everything that exalts itself.

    HERODOTUS ◆ C. 485–C. 425 B.C.E.
    *Histories* VII, 10

15. Abuse of power comes as no surprise.

    JENNY HOLZER ◆ 1950–
    *Truisms*

16. An honest man can feel no pleasure in the exercise
    of power over his fellow citizens.

    THOMAS JEFFERSON ◆ 1743–1826
    Letter to John Melish, January 13, 1813

17. I am tired of an office where I can do no more good
    than many others who would be glad to be employed

in it. To myself, personally, it brings nothing but unceasing drudgery and daily loss of friends.

THOMAS JEFFERSON ◆ 1743–1826
Letter to John Dickinson

18. No man will ever bring out of the Presidency the reputation which carries him into it.

THOMAS JEFFERSON ◆ 1743–1826
Letter to Edward Rutledge

19. That you have enemies you must not doubt, when you reflect that you have made yourself eminent.

THOMAS JEFFERSON ◆ 1743–1826
Letter to James Steptoe

20. I have never been able to conceive how any rational being could propose happiness to himself from the exercise of power over others.

THOMAS JEFFERSON ◆ 1743–1826
Letter to Destutt Tracy

21. Force cannot give right.

THOMAS JEFFERSON ◆ 1743–1826
*The Rights of British America*

22. The nearer we come to great men the more clearly we see that they are only men. They rarely seem great to their valets.

JEAN DE LA BRUYÈRE ◆ 1645–1696
*Caractères*

23. One of the most dangerously vicious circles menacing the continued existence of all mankind arises through that grim striving for the highest possible position within the ranked order....

> KONRAD LORENZ ◆ 1903–1989
> *The Waning of Humaneness*

24. I see it is impossible for the King to have things done as cheap as other men.

> SAMUEL PEPYS ◆ 1633–1703
> *Diary,* July 21, 1662

25. Unlimited power is apt to corrupt the minds of those who possess it.

> WILLIAM PITT ◆ 1759–1806
> Address at the House of Lords, January 9, 1770

26. That individuals have soared above the plane of their race is scarcely to be questioned; but, in looking back through history for traces of their existence we should pass over all biographies of "the good and the great," while we search carefully the slight records of wretches who died in prison, in Bedlam, or upon the gallows.

> EDGAR ALLAN POE ◆ 1809–1849
> *Marginalia*

27. Nearest the king, nearest the gallows.

> *Danish Proverb*

28. He who is feared by many must fear many.

> PUBLILIUS SYRUS ◆ C. 100 B.C.E.
> *Sententiae*

29. I never could believe that Providence had sent a few men into the world, ready booted and spurred to ride, and millions ready saddled and bridled to be ridden.

> RICHARD RUMBOLD ◆ 1622–1685
> Speech on the scaffold

30. O mighty Caesar! dost thou lie so low?
    Are all thy conquests, glories, triumphs, spoils,
    Shrunk to this little measure?

> WILLIAM SHAKESPEARE ◆ 1564–1616
> *Julius Caesar* III, i, 148

31. Uneasy lies the head that wears a crown.

> WILLIAM SHAKESPEARE ◆ 1564–1616
> *King Henry IV Part 2*, III, I

32. What infinite heart's ease
    Must kings neglect that private men enjoy!
    And what have kings that privates have not too,
    Save ceremony, save general ceremony?...

> WILLIAM SHAKESPEARE ◆ 1564–1616
> *King Henry V*, IV, i, 256

33. Tis not the balm, the scepter and the ball,
    The sword, the mace, the crown imperial,
    The intertissued robe of gold and pearl,
    The farced title running 'fore the king,
    The throne he sits on, nor the tide of pomp
    That beats upon the high shore of this world,
    No, not all these, thrice-gorgeous ceremony,
    Not all these, laid in bed majestical,

Can sleep so soundly as the wretched slave,
Who with a body fill'd and vacant mind
Gets him to rest, cramm'd with distressful bread.

*Ibid.*, i, 280

34. What is pomp, rule, reign, but earth and dust?
    And, live we how we can, yet die we must.

WILLIAM SHAKESPEARE ◆ 1564–1616
*King Henry VI Part 3*, V, ii, 27

35. How wretched
    Is that poor man that hangs on princes' favours!
    There is, betwixt that smile we would aspire to,
    That sweet aspect of princes, and their ruin,
    More pangs and fears than wars and women have:
    And when he falls, he falls like Lucifer,
    Never to hope again.

WILLIAM SHAKESPEARE ◆ 1564–1616
*King Henry VIII*, III, ii

36. Farewell! a long farewell, to all my greatness!
    This is the state of man: today he puts forth
    The tender leaves of hope; tomorrow blossoms,
    And bears his blushing honors thick upon him:
    The third day comes a frost, a killing frost,
    And, when he thinks, good easy man, full surely
    His greatness is a-ripening, nips his root,
    And then he falls, as I do.

*Ibid.*, III, ii, 352

37. Had I but serv'd my God with half the zeal
    I serv'd my king, he would not in mine age
    Have left me naked to mine enemies.

*Ibid.*, III, ii, 456

38. Mad world! mad kings! mad composition!

> WILLIAM SHAKESPEARE ◆ 1564–1616
> *King John* II, i, 561

39. For God's sake, let us sit upon the ground
    And tell sad stories of the death of kings:
    How some have been depos'd, some slain in war,
    Some haunted by the ghosts they have depos'd,
    Some poison'd by their wives, some sleeping kill'd;
    All murder'd: for within the hollow crown
    That rounds the mortal temples of a king
    Keeps Death his court.

> WILLIAM SHAKESPEARE ◆ 1564–1616
> *King Richard II,* III, ii, 152

40. They that stand high have many blasts to shake them;
    And if they fall, they dash themselves to pieces.

> WILLIAM SHAKESPEARE ◆ 1564–1616
> *King Richard III,* I, iii

41. Power, like a desolating pestilence,
    Pollutes whate'er it touches.

> PERCY BYSSHE SHELLEY ◆ 1792–1822
> *Queen Mab*

42. If forced to choose between the penitentiary and
    the White House for four years, I would say the
    penitentiary, thank you.

> W(ILLIAM) T(ECUMSEH) SHERMAN ◆ 1820–1891
> Letter to H.W. Halleck, September 1864

43. But I have noticed this about ambitious men, or men in power—they fear even the slightest and least likely threat to it.

MARY STEWART ◆ 1916–
*The Crystal Cave*

44. Lust for power is the most flagrant of all the passions.

(CORNELIUS) TACITUS ◆ C. 56–117
*Annals* II

45. A man in his right mind would never want to be President, if he knew what it entails. Aside from the impossible administrative burden, he has to take all sorts of abuse from liars and demagogues.... All the President is, is a glorified public relations man who spends his time flattering, kissing and kicking people to get them to do what they are supposed to do anyway.

HARRY S. TRUMAN ◆ 1884–1972
Letter to his sister

46. Let...individuals make the most of what God has given them, have their neighbors do the same, and then do all they can to serve each other. There is no use in one man, or one nation, to try to do or be everything. It is a good thing to be dependent on each other for something, it makes us civil and peaceable

SOJOURNER TRUTH ◆ C. 1797–1883
Quoted in Elizabeth Cady Stanton, *History of Woman Suffrage*

47. By the time a man gets to be Presidential material he's been bought ten times over.

GORE VIDAL ◆ 1925–
Quoted in *Newsweek,* November 18, 1974

48. What a dreadful thing it is for such a wicked little imp as man to have absolute power!

HORACE WALPOLE ◆ 1717–1797
Letter to William Mason, July 4, 1778

49. The minute you want to keep power—you've become subservient, somebody who does work you don't believe in.

PAULA WEINSTEIN ◆ 1945–
Quoted in Suzanne Levine and Harriet Lyons, *The Decade of Women*

50. None think the great unhappy, but the great.

EDWARD YOUNG ◆ 1683–1765
*Love of Fame* I

## PHILOSOPHICAL ARGUMENTS

51. A friend in power is a friend lost.

HENRY ADAMS ◆ 1838–1918
*The Education of Henry Adams*

52. The rule of Bolshevism is based on the possession of power. Thus its fate is sealed. While this party and its friends see ultimate goals which are the same as ours, the intoxication of power has seduced them.... Fair becomes foul, foul becomes fair.

ALFRED ADLER ◆ 1870–1937
"Bolshevism and Psychology,"
*The Collected Clinical Works of Alfred Adler*

53. I do not see what it makes for the safety, good morals, and certainly not for the dignity, of men, that some have conquered and others have been conquered, except that it yields them that most insane pomp of human glory, in which "they have received their reward" who burned with excessive desire of it and carried on most eager wars.

SAINT AUGUSTINE ◆ 354–430
*City of God* V, 17

54. Men in great place are thrice servants: servants of the sovereign or state, servants of fame, and servants of business. So as they have no freedom, neither in their persons, nor in their actions, nor in their times. It is a strange desire to seek power and to lose liberty; or to seek power over others and to lose power over a man's self.

FRANCIS BACON ◆ 1561–1626
"Of Great Place," *Essays*

55. However, let us examine this much lauded and much sought after power of yours. You creatures of earth, don't you stop to consider the people over whom you think you exercise authority? You would laugh if you saw a community of mice and one mouse arrogating to himself power and jurisdiction over the others.

(ANICUS MANLIUS SEVERINUS) BOETHIUS C. 480–524
*The Consolation of Philosophy* II, VI

56. But it is said, when a man comes to high office, that makes him worthy of honour and respect. Surely such offices don't have the power of planting virtue in the minds of those who hold them, do they? Or

of removing vices? No: the opposite is true. More often than removing wickedness, high office brings it to light, and this is the reason why we are angry at seeing how often high office has devolved upon the most wicked of men....Surely you can see how much disgrace high office heaps upon the evil? If they don't become famous because of appointments to high office, their unworthiness will be less conspicuous.

*Ibid.*

57. For distant India tremble may
Beneath your mighty rule,
And Thulé bow beneath your sway
Far in the Northern sea,
But if to care and want you're prey,
No king are you, but slave.

*Ibid.*

58. What a splendid thing power is, when we find it insufficient even for its own preservation!

Dionysius the Tyrant of Syracuse knew well enough the dangers of his position, when he illustrated the fears of kingship to Damocles by making a sword dangle over his head by a single hair.

What is this power, then, which cannot banish the nagging of worry or avoid the pin-prick of fear? Kings would like to live free from worry, but they can't. And then they boast of their power! Do you think of a man as powerful when you see him lacking something which he cannot achieve? A man who goes about with a bodyguard because he is more afraid than the subjects he terrorizes, and whose claim to power depends on the will of those who serve him?

Ibid.

59. What sort of power is it, then, that strikes fear into those who possess it, confers no safety on you if you want it, and which cannot be avoided when you want to renounce it?

Ibid.

60. Many do not know that we are here in this world to live in harmony. Those who know this do not fight against each other.

BUDDHA (SIDDHARTHA GAUTAMA) ◆ C. 563–483 B.C.E.
*The Dhammapada* 1.6

61. Better than power over all the earth, better than going to heaven and better than dominion over the world is the joy of the man who enters the river of life that leads to Nirvana.

Ibid., 13.178

62. Life seems easy for those who shamelessly are bold and self-assertive, crafty and cunning, sensuously selfish, wanton and impure, arrogant and insulting, rotting with corruption. But life seems difficult for those who peacefully strive for perfection, who free from self-seeking are not self-assertive, whose life is pure, who see the light.... But the greatest of all sins is indeed the sin of ignorance. Throw this sin away, O man, and become pure from sin.

Ibid., 18.71

63. He that is down needs fear no fall;
    He that is low no pride;
    He that is humble ever shall
    Have God to be his guide.

    JOHN BUNYAN ◆ 1628–1688
    *Pilgrim's Progress* II

64. Power gradually extirpates from the mind every humane and gentle virtue.

    EDMUND BURKE ◆ 1729–1797
    *A Vindication of Natural Society*

65. Every noble crown is, and on earth will forever be, a crown of thorns.

    THOMAS CARLYLE ◆ 1795–1881
    *Past and Present*

66. After the royal throne comes death; after the dunghill comes the Kingdom of Heaven.

    SAINT JOHN CHRYSOSTOM ◆ C. 345–407
    *Homilies* V

67. The power that makes men terrible is a terror first to its possessors; it smiles and frowns; it flatters and deceives; it lifts up and casts down.

    SAINT CYPRIAN ◆ 200–258
    *The World and Its Vanities*

68. Those who love to be feared, fear to be loved; they themselves are of all people the most abject; some fear them, but they fear every one.

    ST. FRANCIS DE SALES ◆ 1567–1622
    Quoted in Jean-Pierre Camus, *L'Esprit de Saint François de Sales*

69. You shall have joy, or you shall have power, said God; you shall not have both.

RALPH WALDO EMERSON ◆ 1803–1882
*Journals*

70. The President has paid dear for his White House. It has commonly cost him all his peace and the best of his manly attributes. To preserve for a short time so conspicuous an appearance before the world, he is content to eat dust before the real masters who stand erect behind the throne.

RALPH WALDO EMERSON ◆ 1803–1882
"Compensation," *Essays: First Series*

71. A man who causes fear cannot be free from fear.

EPICURUS ◆ 341–270 B.C.E.
*Fragments* 84

72. We must say how best a man will maintain the natural end of life, and how no one will willingly at first aim at public office.

Ibid., 87

73. The lust for power is not rooted in strength but in weakness.

ERICH FROMM ◆ 1900–1980
*Escape from Freedom*

74. Power is not happiness. Security and peace are more to be desired than a name at which nations tremble.

WILLIAM GODWIN ◆ 1756–1836
*An Enquiry Concerning Political Justice*

75. Instead of bringing to the power lover a merciful respite from his addictions, old age is apt to intensify them by making it easier for him to satisfy his cravings on a large scale and in a more spectacular way. That is why in Acton's words, "all great men are bad." Can we therefore be surprised if political action undertaken, in all too many cases not for the public good, but solely or at least primarily to gratify the power lusts of bad men, should prove so often either self-stultifying or downright disastrous?

> ALDOUS HUXLEY ◆ 1894–1963
> *The Perennial Philosophy*

76. Of all social, moral and spiritual problems, that of power is the most chronically urgent and the most difficult of solution. Craving for power is not a vice of the body, consequently knows none of the limitations imposed by a tired or satiated physiology upon gluttony, intemperance and lust. Growing with ever successive satisfaction, the appetite for power can manifest itself indefinitely, without interruption by bodily fatigue or sickness.

> Ibid.

77. If I then, your Lord and Master, have washed your feet; ye also ought to wash one another's feet.

> JESUS ◆ C. 4 B.C.E.–30
> *John* 13:14

78. For whosoever exalteth himself shall be abased; and he that humbleth himself shall be exalted.

> JESUS ◆ C. 4 B.C.E.–30
> *Luke* 14:11

79. If any man desire to be first, the same shall be last of all, and servant of all.

JESUS ♦ C. 4 B.C.E.–30
*Mark* 9:35

80. Ye have heard that it hath been said, An eye for an eye, and a tooth for a tooth: But I say unto you, That ye resist not evil: but whosoever shall smite thee on thy right cheek, turn to him the other also.

JESUS ♦ C. 4 B.C.E.–30
*Matthew* 5:38-39

81. Love your enemies, bless them that curse you, do good to them that hate you, and pray for them which despitefully use you, and persecute you.

Ibid., 5:44; also *Luke* 6:27-28

82. Whosoever therefore shall humble himself as this little child, the same is greatest in the kingdom of heaven.

Ibid., 18:4

83. And whosoever will be chief among you, let him be your servant: Even as the Son of man came not to be ministered unto, but to minister, and to give his life a ransom for many.

Ibid., 20:27-28

84. Neither be ye called masters: for one is your Master, even Christ.

Ibid., 23:10

85. Where love rules, there is no will to power; and where power predominates, there love is lacking. The one is the shadow of the other.

> CARL GUSTAV JUNG ◆ 1875–1961
> *Collected Works* 7

86. That kings should become philosophers, and philosophers kings, can scarcely be expected, nor is it wished, since the enjoyment of power inevitably corrupts the judgment of reason, and perverts its liberty.

> IMMANUEL KANT ◆ 1724–1804
> *Perpetual Peace* II

87. To lead them, but not to master them. This is called profound and secret virtue.

> LAO–TZU ◆ C. 604–C.531 B.C.E.
> *The Way of Lao-tzu*

88. For he that thinks absolute power purifies men's blood, and corrects the baseness of human nature, need read but the history of this, or any age, to be convinced to the contrary.

> JOHN LOCKE ◆ 1632–1704
> *Two Treatises on Government*

89. Nothing is sweeter than to occupy the quiet precincts that are well protected by the teachings of the wise, from where you can look down on others and see them wandering all over the place, getting lost and seeking the way in life, striving by their wits, pitting their noble birth, by night and by day struggling by

superior efforts to rise to power at the top and make all theirs.

LUCRETIUS (TITUS LUCRETIUS) ◆ 99–55 B.C.E.
*On the Nature of Things* II, 1

90. To ask for power is forcing uphill a stone which after all rolls back again from the summit and seeks in headlong haste the levels of the plain.

Ibid., III

91. [W]hoever is the cause of another becoming powerful, is ruined himself; for that power is produced by him either through craft or force; and both of these are suspected by the one who has been raised to power.

NICCOLO MACHIAVELLI ◆ 1469–1527
*The Prince*

92. No matter that we may mount on stilts, we still must walk on our own legs. And on the highest throne in the world, we still sit only on our own bottoms.

MICHEL EYQUEM DE MONTAIGNE ◆ 1533–1592
*Essays* III, 13

93. Experience constantly proves that every man who has power is impelled to abuse it.

CHARLES DE SECONDAT MONTESQUIEU ◆ 1689–1755
*De l'Esprit des Lois* xi. 4

94. Great lords have their pleasures, but the people have fun.

CHARLES DE SECONDAT MONTESQUIEU ◆ 1689–1755
*Pensées Diverses*

95. The secret of happiness is this: let your interests be as wide as possible, and let your reactions to the things and persons that interest you be as far as possible friendly rather than hostile.

BERTRAND RUSSELL ◆ 1872–1970
*The Conquest of Happiness*

96. Those who have seized power, even for the noblest of motives, soon persuade themselves that there are good reasons for not relinquishing it. This is particularly likely to happen if they believe themselves to represent some immensely important cause. They will feel that their opponents are ignorant and perverse; before long they will come to hate them.... The important thing is to keep their power, not to use it as a means to an eventual paradise. And so what were means become ends, and the original ends are forgotten except on Sundays.

BERTRAND RUSSELL ◆ 1872–1970
Review of Crossman's *The God That Failed,* in *Saturday Review,* 1951

97. To be able to endure odium is the first art to be learned by those who aspire to power.

LUCIUS ANNAEUS SENECA ◆ C. 4 B.C.E.–54
*Hercules Furens*

98. Most powerful is he who has himself in his own power.

LUCIUS ANNAEUS SENECA ◆ C. 4 B.C.E.–54
*Moral Essays*

99.  Power takes as ingratitude the writhing of its victims.

> RABINDRANATH TAGORE ◆ 1861–1941
> *Stray Birds* 158

100. Without hypocrisy, lying, punishments, prisons, fortresses and murders, no new power can arise and no existing one hold its own.

> LEO NIKOLAEVICH TOLSTOY ◆ 1828–1910
> *The Kingdom of God is Within You*

101. In order to obtain and hold power a man must love it. Thus the effort to get it is not likely to be coupled with goodness, but with the opposite qualities of pride, craft and cruelty.

> Ibid.

# ARGUMENTS FOR THE PURSUIT OF POWER

## ARGUMENTS FOR THE PURSUIT OF POWER IN ORDER TO DO GOOD

102. Great persons are able to do great kindnesses.

> MIGUEL DE CERVANTES ◆ 1547–1616
> *Don Quixote de la Mancha* II, 3.32

103. On the night of the tenth of May [1940], at the outset of this mighty battle, I acquired the chief power in the State, which henceforth I wielded in ever-growing measure for five years and three months of world

war, at the end of which time, all our enemies having surrendered unconditionally or being about to
do so, I was immediately dismissed by the British
electorate from all further conduct of their affairs.

WINSTON CHURCHILL ♦ 1874–1965
*The Gathering Storm*

104. In men of the highest character and noblest genius
there generally exists insatiable desire of honor,
command, power and glory.

MARCUS TULLIUS CICERO ♦ 106–43 B.C.E.
*De Officiis* 1

105. This is the bitterest pain among men, to have much
knowledge but no power.

HERODOTUS ♦ C. 485 B.C.E.–C. 425 B.C.E.
*Histories* IX, 16

106. Power…is not an end in itself, but is an instrument
that must be used toward an end.

JEANE JORDAN KIRKPATRICK ♦ 1926–
Speech

107. All public power proceeds from God.

POPE LEO XIII ♦ 1810–1903
*Immortale Dei,* November 1, 1885

108. There is a homely adage which runs: "Speak softly
and carry a big stick; you will go far."

THEODORE ROOSEVELT ♦ 1858–1919
Speech at Minnesota State Fair, September 2, 1901

109. Do not get into a fight if you can possibly avoid it. If you get in, see it through. Don't hit if it is honorably possible to avoid hitting, but never hit soft. Don't hit at all if you can help it; don't hit a man if you can possibly avoid it; but if you do hit him, put him to sleep.

THEODORE ROOSEVELT ◆ 1858–1919
Speech in Washington, January 24, 1918

110. Power does not corrupt men: fools, however, if they get into a position of power, corrupt power.

GEORGE BERNARD SHAW ◆ 1856–1950
Quoted in Stephen Winsten, *Days with Bernard Shaw*

111. Who desires peace should prepare for war. (*Qui desiderat pacem, preparet bellum.*)

VEGETIUS (FLAVIUS VEGETIUS RENATUS) ◆ FL. C. 375
Prologue, *De Rei Militari* III

---

ARGUMENTS FOR THE PURSUIT OF POWER
IN ORDER TO ACHIEVE INDEPENDENCE, OR
DEFEND ONESELF

---

112. Deeds of violence in our society are performed largely by those trying to establish their self-esteem, to defend their self-image, and to demonstrate that they, too, are significant.... Violence arises not out of superfluity of power but out of powerlessness.

ROLLO MAY ◆ 1909–1994
*Power and Innocence*

113. The property of power is to protect.

> BLAISE PASCAL ♦ 1623–1662
> *Pensées* 310

114. Most power is illusionary and perceptual. You have to create an environment in which people perceive you as having some power.

> CARRIE SAXON PERRY ♦ 1931–
> Quoted in Brian Lanker, *I Dream a World:*
> *Portraits of Black Women Who Changed America*

115. I do not wish them [women] to have power over men but over themselves.

> MARY WOLLSTONECRAFT ♦ 1759–1797
> *A Vindication of the Rights of Woman*

116. It is vain to expect virtue from women till they are, in some degree, independent of men.... Whilst they are absolutely dependent on their husbands they will be cunning, mean, and selfish, and the men who can be gratified by the fawning fondness of spaniel-like affection, have not much delicacy, for love is not to be bought, in any sense of the words, its silken wings are instantly shrivelled up when any thing beside a return in kind is sought.

> Ibid.

## ARGUMENTS FOR THE PURSUIT OF POWER FOR ITS OWN SAKE

117. Great men are the real men: in them nature has succeeded.

> HENRI FREDERIC AMIEL ◆ 1821–1881
> *Journal,* August 13, 1865

118. Being physically close to extreme power causes one to experience a giddiness, an intoxication.

> MAYA ANGELOU ◆ 1928–
> *All God's Children Need Traveling Shoes*

119. All political questions, all matters of right, are at bottom only questions of might.

> AUGUST BEBEL ◆ 1840–1913
> Reichstag speech, July 3, 1871

120. 'Twere better my enemy envy me than I him.

> HENRY GEORGE BOHN ◆ 1796–1884
> *Handbook of Proverbs*

121. Had I succeeded, I should have died with the reputation of the greatest man that ever existed. As it is, although I have failed, I shall be considered as an extraordinary man. I have fought fifty pitched battles, almost all of which I have gained. I have framed and carried into effect a code of laws that will bear my name to the most distant posterity.

> NAPOLEON I BONAPARTE ◆ 1769–1821
> To Barry E. O'Meara at St. Helena, March 3, 1817

122. Men of my stamp do not commit crimes.

> NAPOLEON I BONAPARTE ◆ 1769–1821
> Quoted in Emerson, "Napoleon; or, the Man of the World,"
> *Representative Men*

123. God is usually on the side of big squadrons against little ones.

> ROGER DE BUSSY-RABUTIN ◆ 1618–1693
> Letter to the Comte de Limoges, October 18, 1667

124. I came, I saw, I conquered. (*Veni, vidi, vici.*)

> JULIUS CAESAR ◆ 100–44 B.C
> Dispatch to the Roman Senate after the Battle of Zela

125. We can't do without dominating others or being served. . . . Even the man on the bottom rung still has his wife, or his child. If he's a bachelor, his dog. The essential thing, in sum, is being able to get angry without the other person being able to answer back.

> ALBERT CAMUS ◆ 1913–1960
> *The Fall*

126. It is a stern business killing of a king. But if you once go to war with him, it lies there; this and all else lies there. Once at war, you have made wager of battle with him: it is he to die, or else you.

> THOMAS CARLYLE ◆ 1795–1881
> *Heroes and Hero Worship* VI

127. It is an absolute impossibility in this society to reversely sexually objectify heterosexual men, just as it is impossible for a poor person of color to be a

racist. Such extreme prejudice must be accompanied by the power of society's approval and legislation. While women and poor people of color may become intolerant, personally abusive, even hateful, they do not have enough power to be racist or sexist.

ANA CASTILLO ◆ 1953–
*Massacre of the Dreamers*

128. Who to himself is law, no law doth need,
Offends no law, and is a king indeed.

GEORGE CHAPMAN ◆ C. 1559–1634
*Bussy D'Ambois* II, i

129. The life of the wolf is the death of the lamb.

JOHN CLARKE ◆ C. 1609–1676
*Paroemiologia Anglo-Latina*

130. Nature has left this tincture in the blood,
That all men would be tyrants if they could.

DANIEL DEFOE ◆ C. 1660–1731
*The History of the Kentish Petition*

131. Power doesn't have to show off. Power is confident, self-assuring, self-starting and self-stopping, self-warming and self-justifying. When you have it, you know it.

RALPH ELLISON ◆ 1914–1994
*The Invisible Man*

132. Life is a search after power; and this is an element with which the world is so saturated,—there is no

chink or crevice in which it is not lodged,—that no honest seeking goes unrewarded

RALPH WALDO EMERSON ◆ 1803-1882
"Power," *The Conduct of Life*

133. We must obey the gods, whatever those gods are.
I say that kings kill, rob, break oaths, lay cities
waste by fraud,
And doing thus are happier than those
Who live calm pious lives day after day.
How many little states that serve the gods
Are subject to the godless but more strong,
Made slaves by might of a superior army!

EURIPIDES ◆ 485–406 B.C.E.
*Orestes*

134. Let not thy will roar when thy power can but whisper.

THOMAS FULLER ◆ 1608-1661
*Introductio ad Prudentiam* I

135. The greatest joy a man can have is victory: to conquer one's enemy's armies, to pursue them, to deprive them of their possessions, to reduce their families to tears, to ride on their horses, and to make love to their wives and daughters.

GENGHIS KHAN ◆ C. 1200-1300
Quoted in *TimeFrame AD 1200-1300: The Mongol Conquests*

136. Ironically, women who acquire power are more likely to be criticized for it than are the men who have always had it.

CAROLYN (AMANDA CROSS) HEILBRUN ◆ 1926–2003
*Writing a Woman's Life*

137. I shall give a propagandist cause for starting the war. Never mind whether it is plausible or not. The victor will not be asked, later on, whether he told the truth or not. In starting and waging a war, it is not Right that matters but Victory. Have no pity. Adopt a brutal attitude.... Right is on the side of the strongest.

ADOLF HITLER ◆ 1889–1945
Speech to high officers, August 22, 1939

138. So that in the first place, I put for a general inclination of all mankind, a perpetual and restless desire of power after power, that ceaseth only in death.

THOMAS HOBBES ◆ 1588–1679
*Leviathan* I, 11

139. To this war of every man against every man, this also is consequent; that nothing can be unjust. The notions of right and wrong, justice and injustice have there no place. Where there is no common power, there is no law, where no law, no injustice. Force and fraud are in war the cardinal virtues.

Ibid., I, 12

140. The only prize much cared for by the powerful is power. The prize of the general is not a bigger tent, but command.

OLIVER WENDELL HOLMES ◆ 1841–1935
Speech to Harvard Law School Association of New York,
February 15, 1913

141. The only way to get along is to seek the difficult job, always do it well, and see that you get paid for

it properly. Oh, yes, and don't forget to exploit men all you can. Because if you don't they will exploit you.

EL DORADO JONES ◆ 1861–1932
Quoted in Anne L. MacDonald, *Feminine Ingenuity*

142. And the talk slid north, and the talk slid south,
With the sliding puffs from the hookah-mouth.
Four things greater than all things are,
—Women and Horses and Power and War.

RUDYARD KIPLING ◆ 1865–1936
*Ballad of the King's Jest*

143. In this world a man must be either anvil or hammer.

HENRY WADSWORTH LONGFELLOW ◆ 1807–1882
*Hyperion* IV

144. In business everyone is out to grab, to fight, to win.
Either you are the under or the over dog. It is up to you to be on top.

ALICE FOOTE MACDOUGALL ◆ 1867–1945
*The Autobiography of a Business Woman*

145. Men do with less remorse offend against those who desire to be beloved than against those who are ambitious of being feared, and the reason is because love is fastened only by a ligament of obligation, which the ill-nature of mankind breaks upon every occasion that is presented to his profit; but fear depends upon an apprehension of punishment, which is never to be dispelled.

NICCOLO MACHIAVELLI ◆ 1469–1527
*The Prince* XVII

146. As a prince must be able to act just like a beast, he should learn from the fox and the lion; because the lion does not defend himself against traps, and the fox does not defend himself against wolves. So one has to be a fox in order to recognize traps, and a lion to frighten off wolves.

Ibid., XVIII

147. I have the same goal I've had ever since I was a girl. I want to rule the world.

MADONNA (CICCONE) ◆ 1958–
Quoted in *People* magazine

148. To such a view aggression, in its primary sense of onward movement, is inevitable. Those who will not move must be swept aside.

ALFRED THAYER MAHAN ◆ 1840–1914
"Armaments and Arbitration," *Harper's*, 1912

149. Power never takes a back step—only in the face of more power.

MALCOLM X ◆ 1925–1965
*Malcolm X Speaks*

150. Every Communist must grasp the truth, "Political power grows out of the barrel of a gun."

MAO TSE-TUNG ◆ 1893–1976
"Problems of War and Strategy," *Selected Works* II, ii, 6

151. Is it not passing brave to be a King,
And ride in triumph through Persepolis?

CHRISTOPHER MARLOWE ◆ 1564–1593
*Tamburlaine the Great* 1.758

152. Better to reign in Hell than serve in Heaven.

> JOHN MILTON ◆ 1608–1674
> *Paradise Lost* I

153. What is happiness?—The feeling that power increases—that resistance is overcome.

> FRIEDRICH WILHELM NIETZSCHE ◆ 1844–1900
> *The Antichrist*

154. I preach not contentedness, but more power; not peace, but war; not virtue, but efficiency. The weak and defective shall perish; and they shall be given assistance: that is the first principle of the dionysian charity.

> Ibid.

155. What is bad? All that proceeds from weakness.

> Ibid.

156. Where the will to power is wanting, there is decline.

> Ibid.

157. It is the business of the very few to be independent; it is a privilege of the strong.

> FRIEDRICH WILHELM NIETZSCHE ◆ 1844–1900
> *Beyond Good and Evil*

158. Wherever I found a living creature, there I found the will to power.

> FRIEDRICH WILHELM NIETZSCHE ◆ 1844–1900
> *Thus Spake Zarathustra*

159. The famous struggle for existence seems to me to be more of an assumption than a fact. It does occur, but only as an exception. The general condition of life is not one of want or famine, but rather one of riches, of lavish luxuriance, and even of absurd prodigality. Where there is a struggle, it is a struggle for power.

FRIEDRICH WILHELM NIETZSCHE ◆ 1844–1900
*The Twilight of the Idols*

160. Every high degree of power always involves a corresponding degree of freedom from good and evil.

FRIEDRICH WILHELM NIETZSCHE ◆ 1844–1900
*The Will to Power*

161. I feel that the true way of dealing with the matter is by a force which is overwhelming and prevents any attempt at resistance.

RICHARD OLNEY ◆ 1835–1917
Instructions to Edwin Walker, special U.S. district attorney,
during the Pullman Strike, June 30, 1894

162. Might is right, and justice is the interest of the stronger.

PLATO ◆ C. 428–348 B.C.E.
*The Republic* I

163. The more might, the more right.

PLAUTUS ◆ C. 254–184 B.C.E.
*Truculentus*

164. Providence is always on the side of the battalions.

MARIE DE RABUTIN–CHANTAL (MARQUISE DE SEVIGNE) ◆ 1626–1696
*Letters of Madame de Sevigne to Her Daughter and Her Friends*

165. Popular culture entered my life as Shirley Temple, who was exactly my age and wrote a letter in the newspapers telling how her mother fixed spinach for her, with lots of butter. . . . I was impressed by Shirley Temple as a little girl my age who had power: she could write a piece for the newspapers and have it printed in her own handwriting.

> ADRIENNE RICH ◆ 1929–
> *What Is Found There*

166. A sense of power is the most intoxicating stimulant a mortal can enjoy. . . .

> ELLEN HENRIETTA SWALLOW RICHARDS ◆ 1842–1911
> Quoted in Caroline L. Hunt, *The Life of Ellen H. Richards*

167. This is the Law of the Yukon, that only the Strong
    shall thrive;
  That surely the Weak shall perish, and only the Fit
    survive.
  Dissolute, damned, and despairful, crippled and
    palsied and slain,
  This is the Will of the Yukon,
    —Lo! how she makes it plain!

> ROBERT W. SERVICE ◆ 1874–1958
> "The Law of the Yukon," *Songs of a Sourdough*

168. A scepter snatch'd with an unruly hand
  Must be as boisterously maintain'd as gain'd;
  And he that stands upon a slippery place
  Makes nice of no vile hold to stay him up.

> WILLIAM SHAKESPEARE ◆ 1564-1616
> *King John* III, iv, 135

169. [H]e doth bestride the narrow world
Like a colossus, and we petty men
Walk under his huge legs.

WILLIAM SHAKESPEARE ◆ 1564–1616
*Julius Caesar* I, ii

170. When beggars die there are no comets seen;
The heavens themselves blaze forth the death of
princes.

Ibid.

171. [F]ishes live in the sea . . . as men do a-land: the great
ones eat up the little ones.

WILLIAM SHAKESPEARE ◆ 1564–1616
*Pericles* II, i

172. Some are born great, some achieve greatness, and
some have greatness thrust upon them.

WILLIAM SHAKESPEARE ◆ 1564–1616
*Twelfth Night* III, iv

173. How many divisions has the Pope?

JOSEPH STALIN (JOSIF VISSARIONOVICH DZHUGASHVILI) ◆ 1879–1953
Quoted in *The New York Times,* October 8, 1958

174. Power can be taken, but not given. The process of
the taking is empowerment in itself.

GLORIA STEINEM ◆ 1934–
*Outrageous Acts and Everyday Rebellions*

175. The less powerful group usually knows the powerful
one much better than vice versa—blacks have had to
understand whites in order to survive, women have

had to know men—yet the powerful group can afford to regard the less powerful one as a mystery.

Ibid.

176. Anything a powerful group has is perceived as good, no matter what it is, and anything a less powerful group has is not so good, no matter how intrinsically great it might be.

GLORIA STEINEM ◆ 1934–<br>*Moving Beyond Words*

177. Right resolves itself into its natural nothingness when it is swallowed up by force.

MAX STIRNER ◆ 1806–1856<br>*The Ego and His Own*

178. Nature is one with rapine, a harm no preacher can heal;
The mayfly is torn by the swallow, the sparrow speared by the shrike,
And the whole little wood where I sit is a world of plunder and prey.

ALFRED, LORD TENNYSON ◆ 1809–1892<br>*Maud* I

179. Any man, be his name Bill Sykes or Alexander Romanoff, and any set of men, whether the Chinese highbinders or the Congress of the United States, have the right, if they have the power, to kill or coerce other men and to make the entire world subservient to their ends.

BENJAMIN R. TUCKER ◆ 1854–1939<br>*Instead of a Book*

180. Smart tyrants never come to grief.

VOLTAIRE (FRANÇOIS MARIE AROUET) ◆ 1694–1778
*Merope* V

181. Might is right, and justice there is none.

WALTHER VON DER VOGELWEIDE ◆ C. 1170-C. 1230
*Millennium*

# FAME

## ARGUMENTS AGAINST
## THE PURSUIT OF FAME*

### BASIC ARGUMENTS

1.  A celebrity is a person who works hard all his life to become known, then wears dark glasses to avoid being recognized.

    FRED ALLEN (JOHN F. SULLIVAN) ◆ 1894–1956
    *Treadmill to Oblivion*

2.  Fame always brings loneliness. Success is as ice cold and as lonely as the north pole.

    VICKI BAUM ◆ 1888–1960
    *Grand Hotel*

3.  Alas, we are the victims of advertisement. Those who taste the joys and sorrows of fame when they have passed forty, know how to look after themselves.

---

* *Arguments for* ... begin on page 95.

They know what is concealed beneath the flowers, and what the gossip, the calumnies, and the praise are worth. But as for those who win fame when they are twenty, they know nothing, and are caught up in the whirlpool.

SARAH BERNHARDT ◆ 1845–1923
*The Art of the Theatre*

4.  When we are dead, we are dead.

NAPOLEON I BONAPARTE ◆ 1769–1821
To Gaspard Gourgaud at St. Helena, January 10, 1818

5.  [W]e that are Christian Catholick Knights-Errant must fix our Hopes upon a higher Reward, plac'd in the Eternal and Celestial Regions, where we may expect a permanent Honour and compleat Happiness; not like the Vanity of Fame, which at best is but the Shadow of great Actions, and must necessarily vanish, when destructive Time has eat away the Substance which it follow'd.

MIGUEL DE CERVANTES ◆ 1547–1616
*Don Quixote de la Mancha* II, 8

6.  That's what fame is: solitude.

COCO (GABRIELLE BONHEUR) CHANEL ◆ 1883–1971
Quoted in Marcel Haedrich, *Coco Chanel: Her Life, Her Secrets*

7.  No man is a hero to his valet.

ANNE BIGOT CORNUEL ◆ C. 17TH CENTURY
(Attributed)

8.  Fame is but wind.

THOMAS CORYATE ◆ C. 1577–1617
*Crudities*

9. Worldly renown is naught but a breath of wind, which now comes this way and now comes that, and changes name because it changes quarter.

DANTE (DANTE ALIGHIERI) ◆ 1265–1321
"Purgatorio," *The Divine Comedy* 11

10. Fame is a bee.
It has a song—
It has a sting—
Ah, too, it has a wing.

EMILY DICKINSON ◆ 1830–1886
"Fame Is a Bee," *Collected Poems*

11. How dreary—to be—Somebody!
How public—like a Frog—
To tell one's name—the live-long June—
To an admiring Bog!

EMILY DICKINSON ◆ 1830–1886
"Life," *Complete Poems*

12. Fame is a fickle food
Upon a shifting plate.

EMILY DICKINSON ◆ 1830–1886
"The Single Hound," *Complete Poems*

13. From fame to infamy is a beaten road.

THOMAS FULLER ◆ 1654–1734
*Gnomologia*

14. Fame is but the breath of the people, and that often unwholesome.

Ibid.

15. Fame is a magnifying-glass.

Ibid.

16. All fame is dangerous: good bringeth envy; bad, shame.

Ibid.

17. It was on the night of June 27 1787, between the hours of eleven and twelve, that I wrote the last lines of the last page, in a Summerhouse in my garden.... I will not dissemble the first emotions of joy on the recovery of my freedom, and perhaps, the establishment of my fame. But my pride was soon humbled, and a sober melancholy was spread over my mind, by the idea that I had taken an everlasting leave of an old and agreeable companion, and that whatsoever might be the future fate of my History, the life of the historian must be short and precarious.

EDWARD GIBBON ◆ 1737–1794<br>"Memoirs," reference to The Decline and Fall of the Roman Empire

18. Can storied urn or animated bust
Back to its mansion call the fleeting breath?
Can Honour's voice provoke the silent dust,
Or Flatt'ry sooth the dull cold ear of Death?

THOMAS GRAY ◆ 1716–1771<br>Elegy Written in a Country Churchyard

19. Far from the madding crowd's ignoble strife,
Their sober wishes never learn'd to stray;
Along the cool sequester'd vale of life
They kept the noiseless tenor of their way.

Ibid.

20. For a good man fame is always a problem.

GRAHAM GREENE ◆ 1904–1991
*A Burnt-Out Case*

21. Stardom can be a gilded slavery.

HELEN HAYES ◆ 1900–1993
*On Reflection*

22. He who wishes to make a name for himself loses his name....

HILLEL ◆ C. 30 B.C.E.–10
*Babylonian Talmud,* Avoth i, 13

23. Fame usually comes to those who are thinking about something else.

OLIVER WENDELL HOLMES ◆ 1809–1894
*The Autocrat of the Breakfast-Table*

24. Ah, pensive scholar, what is fame?
    A fitful tongue of leaping flame;
    A giddy whirlwind's fickle gust,
    That lifts a pinch of mortal dust;
    A few swift years, and who can show
    What dust was Bill and which was Joe?

OLIVER WENDELL HOLMES ◆ 1809–1894
*Bill and Joe*

25. Nor has he lived ill, who from birth to death has passed unknown.

HORACE (QUINTUS HORATIUS) ◆ 65–8 B.C.E.
*Epistles* I, xvii, 1. 9

26. He is happiest of whom the world says least, good or bad.

Thomas Jefferson ◆ 1743–1826
Letter to John Adams

27. Then on the shore
Of the wide world I stand alone, and think
Till love and fame to nothingness do sink.

John Keats ◆ 1795–1821
*When I Have Fears*

28. The more I had won that year, the less it meant … and the more tired and sad I became. And the more I won, the more people wanted a part of me. I will tell you King's First Law of Recognition: You never get it when you want it, and then when it comes, you get too much.

Billie Jean King ◆ 1943–
*Billie Jean*

29. On any morning these days whole segments of the population wake up to find themselves famous, while, to keep matters shipshape, whole contingents of celebrities wake up to find themselves forgotten.

Louis Kronenberger ◆ 1904–1980
"The Spirit of the Age," *Company Manners*

30. The boy who hankers after fame has no idea what fame is.

Milan Kundera ◆ 1929–
*The Unbearable Lightness of Being*

31.  He who disdains fame enjoys it in its purity.

> LIVY (TITUS LIVIUS) ◆ 59 B.C.E.–17
> *History of Rome* XXII

32.  Fame is a revenue payable only to our ghosts.

> GEORGE MACKENZIE ◆ 1630–1714
> "A Moral Essay, Preferring Solitude to Publick Employment"

33.  I do not like the man who squanders life for fame.

> MARTIAL (MARCUS VALERIUS MARTIALIS) ◆ C. 40–C. 104
> *Epigrams* I, 86

34.  When I hear a man applauded by the mob I always feel a pang of pity for him. All he has to do to be hissed is to live long enough.

> H(ENRY) L(OUIS) MENCKEN ◆ 1880–1956
> *Minority Report*

35.  People feel fame gives them some kind of privilege to walk up to you and say anything to you, of any kind of nature—and it won't hurt your feelings—like it's happening to your clothing.

> MARILYN MONROE ◆ 1926–1962
> Quoted in *Ms.* magazine

36.  Fame's carapace does not allow for easy breathing.

> JOYCE CAROL OATES ◆ 1938–
> "Pseudonymous Selves," *(Woman) Writer: Occasions and Opportunities*

37.  I was the toast of two continents: Greenland and Australia.

> DOROTHY PARKER ◆ 1893–1967
> Quoted in John Keats, *You Might As Well Live:*
> *The Life and Times of Dorothy Parker*

38.  We are so presumptuous that we wish to be known by all the world, and even by people who will live after we are gone; and we are so vain that the good opinion of five or six persons near us delights and contents us.

> BLAISE PASCAL ♦ 1623–1662
> *Pensées* II

39.  And what is fame?
The meanest have their day;
The greatest can but blaze and pass away.

> ALEXANDER POPE ♦ 1688–1744
> *The First Epistle of the First Book of Horace*

40.  Fame can never make us lie down contentedly on a deathbed.

> ALEXANDER POPE ♦ 1688–1744
> Letter to William Trumbull, March 12, 1713

41.  Nor fame I slight, nor for her favors call;
She comes unlooked for, if she comes at all.

> ALEXANDER POPE ♦ 1688–1744
> *The Temple of Fame*

42.  Sometimes it takes years to really grasp what has happened to your life. What do you do after you are world-famous and nineteen or twenty and you have sat with prime ministers, kings and queens, the Pope? What do you do after that? Do you go back home and take a job? What do you do to keep your sanity? You come back to the real world.

> WILMA RUDOLPH ♦ 1940–1994
> Quoted in Brian Lanker, *I Dream a World:*
> *Portraits of Black Women Who Changed America*

43.  So this was fame at last! Nothing but a vast debt to be paid to the world in energy, blood, in time.

> MAY SARTON ♦ 1912–1995
> *Mrs. Stevens Hears the Mermaids Singing*

44.  There's hope a great man's memory may outlive his life half a year.

> WILLIAM SHAKESPEARE ♦ 1564–1616
> *Hamlet* III, ii

45.  The evil that men do lives after them,
The good is oft interred with their bones.

> WILLIAM SHAKESPEARE ♦ 1564–1616
> *Julius Caesar* III, ii, 79

46.  A plague on eminence! I hardly dare cross the street any more without a convoy, and I am stared at wherever I go like an idiot member of a royal family or an animal in a zoo; and zoo animals have been known to die from stares.

> IGOR STRAVINSKY ♦ 1882–1971
> Quoted in *The New York Review of Books,* May 12, 1966

47.  There is no faster way of destroying a man, or mocking his ideas, than making him fashionable.

> PAUL THEROUX ♦ 1941–
> *The Old Patagonian Express*

48.  What a heavy burden is a name that becomes famous too soon.

> VOLTAIRE (FRANÇOIS MARIE AROUET) ♦ 1694–1778
> *La Henriade* III

49.  Vain the ambition of kings
     Who seek by trophies and dead things
     To leave a living name behind,
     And weave but nets to catch the wind.

> JOHN WEBSTER ◆ C. 1580–1625
> *The Devil's Law-Case* V, iv

---

## PHILOSOPHICAL ARGUMENTS

---

50.  Life is warfare and a pilgrim's brief sojourn, and
     fame after death is only forgetfulness.

> MARCUS AURELIUS ANTONINUS ◆ 121–180
> *Meditations* II, 17

51.  All is ephemeral—fame and the famous as well.

> Ibid., IV, 35

52.  Consider how many do not even know your name
     and how many will soon forget it, and how those who
     now praise you will presently blame you. Fame after
     death is of no value, and neither is reputation now,
     nor anything else.

> Ibid., IX, 30

53.  The desire for fame tempts even noble minds.

> SAINT AUGUSTINE ◆ 354–430
> *City of God* V

54.  Consider how thin ... fame is and how unimportant.
     It is well known, and you have seen it demonstrated
     by astronomers, that beside the extent of the heav-
     ens, the circumference of the earth has the size of

a point; that is to say, compared with the magnitude of the celestial sphere, it may be thought of as having no extent at all. The surface of the world, then, is small enough, and of it, as you have learnt from the geographer Ptolemy, approximately one quarter is inhabited by living beings known to us. If from this quarter you subtract in your mind all that is covered by sea and marshes and the vast area made desert by lack of moisture, then scarcely the smallest of regions is left for men to live in. This is the tiny point within a point, shut in and hedged about, in which you think of spreading your fame and extending your renown, as if a glory constricted within such tight and narrow confines could have any breadth or splendour. Remember, too, that this same narrow enclosure in which we live is the home of many nations which differ in language, customs and their whole way of life.

(ANICUS MANLIUS SEVERINUS) BOETHIUS ◆ C. 480–524
*The Consolation of Philosophy* II, vii

55. When you think of your future fame you think you are creating for yourself a kind of immortality. But if you think of the infinite recesses of eternity you have little cause to take pleasure in any continuation of your name.... However protracted the life of your fame, when compared with unending eternity it is shown to be not just little, but nothing at all.

Ibid.

56. What do they care about reputation when the body grows lifeless in death which ends all things? If the whole of man dies, body and soul—a belief which

our reason forbids us—fame is nothing at all, since the man who is said to have won it doesn't exist. But if the mind stays conscious when it is freed from the earthly prison and seeks out heaven in freedom, surely it will despise every earthly affair.

Ibid.

57. You, however, don't know how to act uprightly except with an eye to popular favour and empty reputation. You ignore those excellent qualities, a good conscience and virtue, and pursue your reward in the common gossip of people.

Ibid.

58. There must of necessity be many peoples to whom the reputation of one single man can never extend, so that you may consider a man famous, whom the next quarter of the globe will never even have heard of. This is why I don't consider popularity worth mentioning...; its acquisition is fortuitous and its retention continuously uncertain.

Ibid., III, vi

59. Happy the man who, unknown to the world, lives content with himself in some retired nook, whom the love of this nothing called fame has never intoxicated with its vain smoke; who makes all his pleasure dependent on his liberty of action, and gives an account of his leisure to no one but himself.

NICOLAS BOILEAU • 1636–1711
*Epitres* VI

60. Every hero becomes a bore at last. Perhaps Voltaire was not bad-hearted, yet he said of the good Jesus, even, "I pray you, let me never hear that man's name again."

RALPH WALDO EMERSON ◆ 1803–1882
*Representative Men* I

61. The wise man thinks of fame just enough to avoid being despised.

EPICURUS ◆ 341–270 B.C.E.
*Aphorisms*

62. I was never anxious to please the mob. For what pleased them, I did not know, and what I did know, was far removed from their comprehension.

EPICURUS ◆ 341–270 B.C.E.
*Fragments* 43

63. Live unknown.

Ibid., 86

64. Fame and tranquility can never be bedfellows.

MICHEL EYQUEM DE MONTAIGNE ◆ 1533–1592
*Essays* I, 39

65. We care more that people should speak of us than how they speak of us; and it is enough for us that our name should be current in men's mouths, no matter in what way it may be current. It seems that to be known is to have one's life and duration somehow in the keeping of others.

Ibid., II, 16

66. The dispersing and scattering our names into many mouths, we call making them more great.

Ibid.

67. Would you be known by everybody? Then you know nobody.

PUBLILIUS SYRUS ◆ C. 100 B.C.E.<br>*Sententiae* 979

68. The highest form of vanity is love of fame. It is a passion easy to deride but hard to understand, and in men who live at all by imagination almost impossible to eradicate. The good opinion of posterity can have no possible effect on our fortunes, and the practical value which reputation may temporarily have is quite absent in posthumous fame. The direct object of this passion—that a name should survive in men's mouths to which no adequate idea of its original can be attached—seems a thin and fantastic satisfaction, especially when we consider how little we should probably sympathise with the creatures that are to remember us.... Yet, beneath this desire for nominal longevity, apparently so inane, there may lurk an ideal ambition of which the ancients cannot have been unconscious when they set so high a value on fame. They often identified fame with immortality, a subject on which they had far more rational sentiments than have since prevailed.

GEORGE SANTAYANA ◆ 1863–1952<br>*Life of Reason* II, 6

69. Fame has also this great drawback, that if we pursue it we must direct our lives in such a way as to please

the fancy of men, avoiding what they dislike and seeking what is pleasing to them.

BARUCH SPINOZA ✦ 1632–1677
*On the Improvement of the Understanding*

# ARGUMENTS FOR THE PURSUIT OF FAME

## BASIC ARGUMENTS

70. There may be wonder in money, but, dear God, there is money in wonder.

ENID BAGNOLD ✦ 1889–1981
*National Velvet*

71. I awoke one morning and found myself famous.

GEORGE NOEL GORDON, LORD BYRON ✦ 1788–1824
After the publication of *Childe Harold*

72. May [my book] live and last for more than one century.

GAIUS VALERIUS CATULLUS ✦ 87–C. 54 B.C.E.
*Carmina* I, 1, 10

73. And gladder ought a friend be of his death
When, in much honour, he yields up his breath,
Than when his name's grown feeble with old age;
For all forgotten, then, is his courage.
Hence it is best for all of noble name
To die when at the summit of their fame.

GEOFFREY CHAUCER ✦ 1343–1400
"Knight's Tale," *Canterbury Tales*

74. The man who spends his life without winning fame
    leaves such mark of himself on earth as smoke in
    air or foam on water.

    DANTE (DANTE ALIGHIERI) ◆ 1265–1321
    "Inferno," *The Divine Comedy* XXIV

75. The legacy of heroes—the memory of a great name,
    and the inheritance of a great example.

    BENJAMIN DISRAELI ◆ 1804–1881
    Speech in the House of Commons, February 1, 1849

76. Let us now praise famous men.

    *Ecclesiasticus* 44:1 (Apocrypha)

77. When good men die their goodness does not perish,
    But lives though they are gone. As for the bad, All
    that was theirs dies and is buried with them.

    EURIPIDES ◆ 485–406 B.C.E.
    *Temenidae,* fragment 734

78. He hath not lived that lives not after death.

    GEORGE HERBERT ◆ 1593–1633
    *Outlandish Proverbs*

79. I too shall lie in the dust when I am dead, but now
    let me win noble renown.

    HOMER ◆ 8TH CENT. B.C.E.
    *The Iliad* XVIII, 1, 120

80. Therefore the fame of her excellence will never per-
    ish, and the immortals will fashion among earthly
    men a gracious song in honor of faithful Penelope.

    HOMER ◆ 8TH CENT. B.C.E.
    *The Odyssey* XXIV, 1, 196

81.  I have built a monument more lasting than bronze.

> HORACE (QUINTUS HORATIUS)  ◆  65–8 B.C.E.
> *Odes* III, xxx, 1, 1

82.  I shall not wholly die.

> Ibid., 1, 6

83.  Many brave men lived before Agamemnon; but all are overwhelmed in eternal night, unwept, unknown, because they lack a sacred poet.

> Ibid., IV, ix, 1, 25

84.  Contempt of fame begets contempt of virtue.

> BEN JONSON  ◆  1573–1637
> *Sejanus* I

85.  Actors, politicians, and writers—all of us are but creatures of the hour. Long-lasting fame comes to but few.

> LOUIS L'AMOUR  ◆  1908–1988
> *Education of a Wandering Man*

86.  Fame is the advantage of being known by people of whom you yourself know nothing, and for whom you care as little.

> STANISLAUS LESZCYNSKI  ◆  1677–1766
> *Oeuvres du philosophe bienfaisant*

87.  Lives of great men all remind us
We can make our lives sublime,
And departing, leave behind us
Footprints on the sands of time.

> HENRY WADSWORTH LONGFELLOW  ◆  1807–1882
> "A Psalm of Life"

88. What Malherbe writes will endure forever.

> FRANÇOIS DE MALHERBE ♦ 1555–1628
> "Sonnet à Louis XIII"

89. Every warrior . . . is rapt with love
    Of fame, of valour, and of victory.

> CHRISTOPHER MARLOWE ♦ 1564–1593
> *Tamburlaine the Great* 1.1941

90. I was going to get myself recognized at any price. . . . If
    I could not win fame by goodness, I was ready to do
    it by badness. . . .

> MARY MCCARTHY ♦ 1912–1989
> *Memories of a Catholic Girlhood*

91. Fame is the spur that the clear spirit doth raise
    (That last infirmity of Noble mind)
    To scorn delights, and live laborious dayes. . . .

> JOHN MILTON ♦ 1608–1674
> *Lycidas* 70

92. See the conquering hero comes!
    Sound the trumpet, beat the drums!

> THOMAS MORELL ♦ 1703–1784
> *Judas Maccabaeus*

93. And now I have finished a work that neither the
    wrath of love, nor fire, nor the sword, nor devouring
    age shall be able to destroy.

> OVID (PUBLIUS OVIDIUS NASO) ♦ 43 B.C.E.–C. 18
> *Metamorphoses* XV, 871

94. The love of fame puts spurs to the mind.

> OVID (PUBLIUS OVIDIUS NASO) ◆ 43 B.C.E.–C. 18
> *Tristia* V

95. How sweet it is to have people point and say, "There he is."

> PERSIUS (AULUS PERSIUS FLACCUS) ◆ 34–62
> *Satires* I

96. Men are generally more pleased with a widespread than with a great reputation.

> PLINY THE YOUNGER (GAIUS PLINIUS
> CAECILIUS SECUNDUS) ◆ C. 61–C. 112
> *Letters* IV

97. Mankind differ in their notions of happiness; but in my opinion he truly possesses it who lives in the anticipation of honest fame, and the glorious figure he shall make in the eyes of posterity.

> Ibid., IX

98. The only real life is the life of fame.

> *Sanskrit Proverb*

99. Love of fame is the last thing even learned men can bear to be parted from.

> (CORNELIUS) TACITUS ◆ C. 56–117
> *Histories* IV, 6

100. As long as rivers shall run down to the sea, or shadows touch the mountain slopes, or stars graze in the

vault of heaven, so long shall your honor, your name, your praises endure.

VIRGIL (PUBLIUS VERGILIUS MARO) ♦ 70–19 B.C.E.
*Aeneid* I, 1. 607

101. You know when there's a star, like in show business, the star has her name in lights on the marquee! Right? And the star gets the money because the people come to see the star, right? Well, I'm the star, and all of you are in the chorus.

BABE DIDRIKSON ZAHARIAS ♦ 1911–1956
Quoted in *WomenSports* magazine, December 1977

## PHILOSOPHICAL ARGUMENTS

102. I bequeath my soul to God.... My body to be buried obscurely. For my name and memory, I leave it to men's charitable speeches, and to foreign nations, and the next age.

FRANCIS BACON ♦ 1561–1626
*Essays from His Will*

103. He had no failings which were not owing to a noble cause; to an ardent, generous, perhaps an immoderate passion for fame; a passion which is the instinct of all great souls.

EDMUND BURKE ♦ 1729–1797
Said of Charles Townshend, speech on American Taxation

104. Worship of a hero is transcendent admiration of a great man.

THOMAS CARLYLE ♦ 1795–1881
*Heroes and Hero Worship*

105. Hero-worship exists, has existed, and will forever exist, universally among mankind.

THOMAS CARLYLE ◆ 1795–1881
*Sartor Resartus* III

106. True fame has real substance and is precisely fashioned. It is not something ephemeral. It is, rather, the unanimous opinion of good men and the verdict of honest judges on an issue of outstanding merit. It is the echo of virtue's voice. Because fame is concerned with duties rightly done, good men do not disdain it. False fame, which tries to pass itself off as the true, is headstrong and thoughtless. It is compounded of faults and errors and seeks only public acclaim. By its counterfeit nature, it tarnishes the luster of real honor.

MARCUS TULLIUS CICERO ◆ 106–43 B.C.E.
*Disputations* III, 2

107. The charm of fame is so great that we like every object to which it is attached, even death.

BLAISE PASCAL ◆ 1623–1662
*Pensées* 158

108. [T]hink only of the ambition of men, and you will wonder at the senselessness of their ways, unless you consider how they are stirred by the love of an immortality of fame. They are ready to run all risks greater far than they would have run for their children, and to spend money and undergo any sort of toil, and even to die, for the sake of leaving behind them a name which shall be eternal.

PLATO ◆ C. 428–348 B.C.E.
*Symposium*

# PRAISE

## ARGUMENTS AGAINST THE PURSUIT OF PRAISE*

---

### BASIC ARGUMENTS

---

1. Admiration is a very short-lived passion, that immediately decays upon growing familiar with its object.

> JOSEPH ADDISON ◆ 1672–1719
> Quoted in *The Spectator*, December 24, 1711

2. Praise out of season, or tactlessly bestowed, can freeze the heart as much as blame.

> PEARL S(YDENSTRICKER) BUCK ◆ 1892–1973
> *To My Daughters, With Love*

3. Expect not praise without envy until you are dead.

> CHARLES CALEB COLTON ◆ 1780–1832
> *The Lacon*

---

* *Arguments for* ... begin on page 113.

4. Do not trust to the cheering, for those very persons would shout as much if you and I were going to be hanged.

OLIVER CROMWELL ♦ 1599–1658
To John Lambert, on their march to the North

5. [The Cranford ladies'] dress is very independent of fashion; as they observe, "What does it signify how we dress here at Cranford, where everybody knows us?" And if they go from home, their reason is equally cogent: "What does it signify how we dress here, where nobody knows us?"

ELIZABETH GASKELL ♦ 1810–1865
*Cranford*

6. He who praises everybody praises nobody.

SAMUEL JOHNSON ♦ 1709–1784
Quoted in Boswell, *Life of Johnson*

7. Praise [and] money are the two powerful corrupters of mankind.

SAMUEL JOHNSON ♦ 1709–1784
To Hester Thrale, October 27, 1783

8. Madam, before you flatter a man so grossly to his face, you should consider whether or not your flattery is worth his having.

SAMUEL JOHNSON ♦ 1709–1784
Remark to Hannah More,
quoted in Mme. d'Arblay (Fanny Burney), *Diary and Letters*, vol. I

9.  To praise princes for virtues they do not possess is to speak evil of them with impunity.

    FRANÇOIS, DUC DE LA ROCHEFOUCAULD ◆ 1613–1680
    *Maxims*

10. In whatever terms people may praise us, they never teach us anything new.

    Ibid.

11. We do not like to praise, and we never praise without a motive. Praise is flattery, artful, hidden, delicate, which gratifies differently him who praises and him who is praised.

    Ibid.

12. I am accounted by some people a good man. How cheap that character is acquired! Pay your debts, don't borrow money, nor twist your kitten's neck off, nor disturb a congregation, etc., your business is done. I know things (thoughts or things, thoughts are things) of myself, which would make every friend I have fly me as a plague patient.

    CHARLES LAMB ◆ 1775–1834
    Letter to Bernard Barton, February 25, 1824

13. We cannot at once catch the applauses of the vulgar and expect the approbation of the wise.

    WALTER SAVAGE LANDOR ◆ 1775–1864
    "Lucullus and Caesar," *Imaginary Conversations*

14. They praise those works, but they're not the ones they read.

    MARTIAL (MARCUS VALERIUS) ◆ C. 40–C. 104
    *Epigrams* IV, xlix

15. Envy bestrides praise.

> PINDAR ◆ C. 518–C. 438 B.C.E.
> "Olympia 2," *Odes*

16. Praise is the beginning of blame.

> *Japanese Proverb*

17. Help me, Lord, for there is not one godly man left…they do but flatter with their lips, and dissemble in their double heart.

> *Psalms* 12:1

18. [B]e thou as chaste as ice, as pure as snow, thou shalt not escape calumny.

> WILLIAM SHAKESPEARE ◆ 1564–1616
> *Hamlet* III, i, 139

19. Discuss unto me; art thou officer?
    Or art thou base, common and popular?

> WILLIAM SHAKESPEARE ◆ 1564–1616
> *King Henry V*, IV, i, 37

20. Men's evil manners live in brass; their virtues
    We write in water.

> WILLIAM SHAKESPEARE ◆ 1564–1616
> *King Henry VIII*, IV, ii, 46

21. You have too much respect upon the world:
    They lose it that do buy it with much care.

> WILLIAM SHAKESPEARE ◆ 1564–1616
> *The Merchant of Venice* I, i, 74

22. Reputation is an idle and most false imposition; oft got without merit, and lost without deserving.

> WILLIAM SHAKESPEARE ◆ 1564–1616
> *Othello* II, iii, 262

## PHILOSOPHICAL ARGUMENTS

23. Whatever is in any way beautiful hath its source of beauty in itself, and is complete in itself; praise forms no part of it. So it is none the worse nor the better for being praised.

> MARCUS AURELIUS ANTONINUS ◆ 121–180
> *Meditations* IV, 20

24. A man makes no noise over a good deed, but passes on to another as a vine to bear grapes again in seasons.

> Ibid., V, 6

25. It is impossible for happiness to consist in honour.... [V]irtue's true reward is happiness itself, for which the virtuous work, whereas if they worked for honour, it would no longer be virtue, but ambition.

> THOMAS AQUINAS ◆ C. 1225–1274
> *Summa Theologica* I–II, 2, 2

26. How he will wish for reputation, for precedence among the monks, for authority in the monasteries and for veneration amongst the people. 'Let householders and hermits, both, think it was I who did that work; and let them ever ask me what they should do or not do.' These are the thoughts of the

fool, puffed up with desire and pride. But one is the path of earthly wealth, and another is the path of Nirvana. Let the follower of Buddha think of this and, without striving for reputation, let him ever strive after freedom.

BUDDHA (SIDDHARTHA GAUTAMA) ◆ C. 563–483 B.C.E.
*The Dhammapada* 5.45

27. Even as a great rock is not shaken by the wind, the wise man is not shaken by praise or by blame.

Ibid., 6.46

28. This is an old saying, Atula, it is not a saying of today: 'They blame the man who is silent, they blame the man who speaks too much, and they blame the man who speaks too little.' No man can escape blame in this world.

Ibid., 17.68

29. Examine the man who lives in misery because he does not shine above other men; who goes about producing himself, pruriently anxious about his gifts and claims; struggling to force everybody, as it were begging everybody for God's sake, to acknowledge him a great man, and set him over the heads of men! Such a creature is among the wretchedest sights seen under this sun.

THOMAS CARLYLE ◆ 1795–1881
*The Hero as King*

30. It is right to praise Agrippinus on this account, that, although he was a man of the highest worth, he never praised himself but blushed even if another praised him.

EPICTETUS ◆ C. 55–135
*Fragments* 21

31. Pay no heed to what any one says of you, for this, in the end, is no concern of yours.

EPICTETUS ◆ C. 55–135
*The Handbook of Epictetus* 50

32. Take heed that ye do not your alms before men, to be seen of them: otherwise ye have no reward of your Father which is in heaven. Therefore when thou doest thine alms, do not sound a trumpet before thee, as the hypocrites do in the synagogues and in the streets, that they may have glory of men. Verily I say unto you, They have their reward. But when thou doest alms, let not thy left hand know what thy right hand doeth: That thine alms may be in secret: and thy Father which seeth in secret himself shall reward thee openly.

JESUS ◆ C. 4 B.C.E.–30
*Matthew* 6:1-4

33. Then shall they deliver you up to be afflicted, and shall kill you: and ye shall be hated of all nations for my name's sake.

Ibid., 24:9

34. Woe unto you, when all men shall speak well of you! For so did their fathers to the false prophets.

JESUS ◆ C. 4 B.C.E.–30
*Luke* 6:26

35. Woe unto you, Pharisees! For ye love the uppermost seats in the synagogues, and greetings in the markets.

Ibid., 11:43

36. Time as it goes round changes the seasons of things. That which was in esteem, falls at length into utter disrepute; and then another thing mounts up and issues out of its degraded state and every day is more and more coveted and blossoms forth high in honour when discovered and is in marvellous repute with men.

    LUCRETIUS (TITUS LUCRETIUS) ◆ 99–55 B.C.E.
    *On the Nature of Things* V

37. Of all the illusions in the world, the most universally received is the concern for reputation and glory, which we espouse even to the point of giving up riches, rest, life, and health, which are effectual and substantial goods, to follow that vain phantom and mere sound that has neither body nor substance.... And of the irrational humors of men, it seems that even the philosophers get rid of this one later and more reluctantly than any other.

    MICHEL EYQUEM DE MONTAIGNE ◆ 1533–1592
    "Not Communicating One's Glory," *Essays* I, 41

38. It might perhaps be excusable for a painter or another artisan, or even for a rhetorician or a grammarian, to toil to acquire a name by his works; but the actions of virtue are too noble in themselves to seek any other reward than from their own worth, and especially to seek it in the vanity of human judgments.

    "Of Glory," Ibid., II, 16

39. Whatever it is, whether art or nature, that imprints in us this disposition to live with reference to others, it does us much more harm than good. We defraud ourselves of our own advantages to make appear-

ances conform with public opinion. We do not care so much what we are in ourselves and in reality as what we are in the public mind. Even the joys of the mind, and wisdom, appear fruitless to us, if they are enjoyed by ourselves alone, if they do not shine forth to the sight and approbation of others.

"Of Vanity," Ibid., III, 9

40. We do not content ourselves with the life we have in ourselves and in our own being; we desire to live an imaginary life in the mind of others, and for this purpose we endeavour to shine. We labour unceasingly to adorn and preserve this imaginary existence and neglect the real. And if we possess calmness, or generosity, or truthfulness, we are eager to make it known, so as to attach these virtues to that imaginary existence. We would rather separate them from ourselves to join them to it; and we would willingly be cowards in order to acquire the reputation of being brave.... We are so presumptuous that we would wish to be known by all the world, even by people who shall come after, when we shall be no more; and we are so vain that the esteem of five or six neighbours delights and contents us.

BLAISE PASCAL ◆ 1623–1662
*Pensées* II, 147–148

41. The savage lives within himself, while social man lives constantly outside himself, and only knows how to live in the opinion of others, so that he seems to receive the consciousness of his own existence merely from the judgment of others concerning him.

JEAN JACQUES ROUSSEAU ◆ 1712–1778
*A Discourse on the Origin of Inequality*

42. It is this desire for being talked about, and this unremitting rage to distinguish ourselves, that we owe the best and worst things we possess; both our virtues and our vices, our science and our errors, our conquerors and our philosophers; that is to say, a great many bad things and a very few good ones.

Ibid.

43. Achievements which serve no materially useful end...will vary in regard to the chances they have of meeting with timely recognition and due appreciation; and their order of precedence, beginning with those who have the greatest chance, will be somewhat as follows: acrobats, circus-riders, balletdancers, jugglers, actors, singers, musicians, composers, poets, architects, painters, sculptors, philosophers.

ARTHUR SCHOPENHAUER ♦ 1788–1860<br>"Position, or a Man's Place in the Estimation of Others,"<br>*The Wisdom of Life and Counsels and Maxims*

44. What utter foolishness it is to be afraid that those who have a bad name can rob you of a good one.

LUCIUS ANNAEUS SENECA ♦ C. 4 B.C.E.–54<br>*Letters to Lucilius* 91

45. Praise shames me, for I secretly beg for it.

RABINDRANATH TAGORE ♦ 1861–1941<br>*Stray Birds* 207

46. He who loves praise, loves temptation.

BISHOP THOMAS WILSON ♦ 1698–1755<br>*Maxims of Piety and of Christianity*

# ARGUMENTS FOR THE PURSUIT OF PRAISE

## BASIC ARGUMENTS

47. A man who does not love praise is not a full man.

HENRY WARD BEECHER ◆ 1813–1887
*Proverbs from Plymouth Pulpit*

48. The advantage of doing one's praising to oneself is that one can lay it on so thick and exactly in the right places.

SAMUEL BUTLER ◆ 1835–1902
*The Way of All Flesh*

49. They that value not praise will never do anything worthy of praise.

THOMAS FULLER ◆ 1654–1734
*Gnomologia*

50. There must be something good in a thing that pleases so many; even if it cannot be explained, it is certainly enjoyed.

BALTASAR GRACIÁN ◆ 1601–1658
*The Art of Worldly Wisdom*

51. Just about the only interruption we don't object to is applause.

SYDNEY JUSTIN HARRIS ◆ 1917–1986
"Why I Don't Write About Politics," *Clearing the Ground*

52. Let a man, as most men do, rate themselves at the highest value they can, yet their true value is no more than it is esteemed by others.

THOMAS HOBBES ♦ 1588–1679
*Leviathan* I, 10

53. It would be a kind of ferocity to reject indifferently all sorts of praise. One should be glad to have that which comes from good men who praise in sincerity things that are really praiseworthy.

JEAN DE LA BRUYÈRE ♦ 1645–1696
*Caractères*

54. He who refuses praise only wants to be praised again.

FRANÇOIS, DUC DE LA ROCHEFOUCAULD ♦ 1613–1680
*Maxims*

55. There is no other way of guarding oneself against flattery than by letting men understand that they will not offend you by speaking the truth; but when everyone can tell you the truth, you lose their respect.

NICCOLO MACHIAVELLI ♦ 1469–1527
*The Prince*

56. People ask you for criticism, but they only want praise.

W(ILLIAM) SOMERSET MAUGHAM ♦ 1874–1965
*Of Human Bondage*

57. [Spartans] are desirous, from the very first, to have their youth susceptible to good and bad repute, to

feel pain at disgrace, and exultation at being commended; and any one who is insensible and unaffected in these respects is thought poor-spirited and of no capacity for virtue.

PLUTARCH ◆ 46–120
"Lysander," *Lives*

58.  I will praise any man that will praise me.

WILLIAM SHAKESPEARE ◆ 1564–1616
*Antony and Cleopatra* II, vi, 88

59.  Our praises are our wages....

WILLIAM SHAKESPEARE ◆ 1564–1616
*The Winter's Tale* I, ii

60.  The sweetest of all sounds is praise.

XENOPHON ◆ 435–354 B.C.E.
*Hiero* I

## PHILOSOPHICAL ARGUMENTS

61.  It is chiefly with honours and dishonours, then, that the proud man is concerned; and at honours that are great and conferred by good men he will be moderately pleased, thinking that he is coming by his own or even less than his own; for there can be no honour that is worthy of perfect virtue, yet he will at any rate accept it since they have nothing greater to bestow on him; but honour from casual people and on trifling grounds he will utterly despise, since it

is not this that he deserves, and dishonour too, since in his case it cannot be just....

ARISTOTLE ◆ 384–322 B.C.E.
*Ethics*

62. Although I do not care immoderately for glory, or, if I dare say so, although I even hate it, inasmuch as I judge it to be antagonistic to the repose which I esteem above all other things, at the same time I never tried to conceal my actions as though they were crimes, nor have I used many precautions against being known, partly because I should have thought it damaging to myself, and partly because it would have given me a sort of disquietude which would again have militated against the perfect repose of spirit which I seek. And forasmuch as having in this way always held myself in a condition of indifference as regards whether I was known or was not known, I have not yet been able to prevent myself from acquiring some sort of reputation, I thought that I should do my best at least to prevent myself from acquiring an evil reputation.

RENÉ DESCARTES ◆ 1596–1650
*Le Discours de la Methode* VI

63. A man's Social Self is the recognition which he gets from his mates. We are not only gregarious animals, liking to be in sight of our fellows, but we have an innate propensity to get ourselves noticed, and noticed favorably, by our kind. No more fiendish punishment could be devised, were such a thing physically possible, than that one should be turned loose in society and remain absolutely unnoticed by all the members

thereof. If no one turned round when we entered, answered when we spoke, or minded what we did, but if every person we met "cut us dead," and acted as if we were non-existing things, a kind of rage and impotent despair would ere long well up in us, from which the cruellest bodily tortures would be a relief; for these would make us feel that, however bad might be our plight, we had not sunk to such a depth as to be unworthy of attention at all.

WILLIAM JAMES ♦ 1842–1910
*Psychology*

64. Praise is always pleasing, let it come from whom, or upon what account it will.

MICHEL EYQUEM DE MONTAIGNE ♦ 1533–1592
*Essays of Vanity*

65. Honour sets all the parts of the body politic in motion, and by its very action connects them; thus each individual advances the public good, while he only thinks of promoting his own interest. True it is that, philosophically speaking, it is a false honour which moves all the parts of the government; but even this false honour is as useful to the public as true honour could possibly be to private persons.

CHARLES DE SECONDAT MONTESQUIEU ♦ 1689–1755
*De l'Esprit des Lois* III, 7

66. A State which would be safe and happy, as far as the nature of man allows, must and ought to distribute honour and dishonour in the right way. And the right way is to place the goods of the soul first and highest in the scale, always assuming temperance to

be the condition of them; and to assign the second place to the goods of the body; and the third place to money and property And if any legislator or state departs from this rule by giving money the place of honour, or in any way preferring that which is really last, may we not say, that he or the state is doing an unholy and unpatriotic thing?

PLATO ◆ C. 428–348 B.C.E.
*Laws* III, 697A

67. Every artist loves applause. The praise of his contemporaries is the most valuable part of his recompense.

JEAN JACQUES ROUSSEAU ◆ 1712–1778
*A Discourse on the Moral Effects of the Arts and Sciences*

68. Nothing in life gives a man so much courage as the attainment or renewal of the conviction that other people regard him with favor; because it means that everyone joins to give him help and protection, which is an infinitely stronger bulwark against the ills of life than anything he can do himself.

ARTHUR SCHOPENHAUER ◆ 1788–1860
"Position, or a Man's Place in the Estimation of Others,"
*The Wisdom of Life and Counsels and Maxims*

69. If people insist that honor is dearer than life itself, what they really mean is that existence and wellbeing are as nothing compared with other people's opinions. Of course, this may be only an exaggerated way of stating the prosaic truth that reputation, that is, the opinion others have of us, is indispensable if we are to make any progress in the world.

Ibid.

# GLORY

## ARGUMENTS AGAINST THE PURSUIT OF GLORY*

### BASIC ARGUMENTS

1. I have saved myself—what care I for that shield?
   Away with it! I'll get another one no worse.[†]

   > ARCHILOCHUS ◆ EARLY 7TH CENTURY B.C.E.
   > *Fragment 6*

2. "There's glory for you!" "I don't know what you mean by 'glory,'" Alice said. "I meant, 'there's a nice knock-down argument for you!'" "But 'glory' doesn't mean 'a nice knock-down argument,'" Alice objected. "When l use a word," Humpty Dumpty said in a rather scornful tone, "it means just what I choose it to mean—neither more nor less."

   > LEWIS CARROLL (CHARLES LUTWIDGE DODSON) ◆ 1832–1898
   > *Through the Looking-Glass*

---

\* *Arguments for* ... begin on page 125.

† Spartan warriors especially were supposed to return from battle either with their shield, or carried "on it," that is, dead. To lose one's shield means one has fled, not acceptable behavior.

3. For that which befalleth the sons of men befalleth beasts; even one thing befalleth them: as the one dieth, so dieth the other; yea, they have all one breath; so that a man hath no preeminence above a beast: for all is vanity.

*Ecclesiastes* 3:19

4. When we examine what glory is, we discover that it is nearly nothing. To be judged by the ignorant and esteemed by imbeciles, to hear one's name spoken by a rabble who approve, reject, love or hate without reason—that is nothing to be proud of.

FREDERICK THE GREAT ♦ 1712–1786
Letter to Voltaire, January 3, 1773

5. The deed is everything, not the glory.

JOHANN WOLFGANG VON GOETHE ♦ 1749–1832
*Faustus* IV

6. How wide the limits stand
Between a splendid and a happy land.

OLIVER GOLDSMITH ♦ C. 1730–1774
*The Deserted Village*

7. The paths of glory lead but to the grave.

THOMAS GRAY ♦ 1716–1771
*Elegy Written in a Country Churchyard*

8. A pride there is of rank—a pride of birth,
A pride of learning, and a pride of purse,
A London pride—in short, there be on earth
A host of prides, some better and some worse;

But of all prides, since Lucifer's attaint
The proudest swells a self-elected saint.

> THOMAS HOOD ◆ 1799–1845
> *Blanca's Dream*

9. There is no road of flowers leading to glory.

> JEAN DE LA FONTAINE ◆ 1621–1695
> *Fables* X

10. He has true glory who despises it.

> LIVY (TITUS LIVIUS) ◆ 59 B.C.E.–17
> *History of Rome* X

11. To the ashes of the dead glory comes too late.

> MARTIAL (MARCUS VALERIUS) ◆ C. 40–C. 104
> *Epigrams* 1.25

12. Who pants for glory finds but short repose;
    A breath revives him, or a breath o'erthrows.

> ALEXANDER POPE ◆ 1688–1744
> *The First Epistle of the Second Book of Horace*

13. For men to search their own glory is not glory.

> *Proverbs* 25:27

14. A cock has great influence on his own dunghill.

> PUBLILIUS SYRUS ◆ C. 100 B.C.E.
> *Sententiae* 357

15. "Come cheer up, my lads, 'tis to glory we steer"
    As the soldier remarked whose post lay in the rear.

> CHRISTINA ROSSETTI ◆ 1830–1894
> *Couplet*

16. Glory is like a circle in the water,
    Which never ceaseth to enlarge itself
    Till by broad spreading it disperse to nought.

    WILLIAM SHAKESPEARE ◆ 1564–1616
    *King Henry VI Part 2*, I, ii, 133

17. I see thy glory like a shooting star
    Fall to the base earth from the firmament.

    WILLIAM SHAKESPEARE ◆ 1564–1616
    *King Richard II*, II, iv, 19

18. A brittle glory shineth in this face:
    As brittle as the glory is the face.

    Ibid., IV, i, 287

19. Like madness is the glory of this life.

    WILLIAM SHAKESPEARE ◆ 1564–1616
    *Timon of Athens* I

20. O! the fierce wretchedness that glory brings us.

    Ibid., IV, ii, 30

21. Avoid shame, but do not seek glory,—nothing so expensive as glory.

    SYDNEY SMITH ◆ 1771–1845
    *Lady Holland's Memoir*

22. Glories like glow-worms, afar off shine bright, But looked to near, have neither heat nor light.

    JOHN WEBSTER ◆ C. 1580–1625
    *The Duchess of Malfi* 4.2

## PHILOSOPHICAL ARGUMENTS

23.  Let the desire of glory be surpassed by the love of righteousness.... [S]o hostile is this vice to pious faith, if the love of glory be greater in the heart than the fear or love of God, that the Lord said, 'How can ye believe, who look for glory from one another, and do not seek the glory which is from God alone?'

SAINT AUGUSTINE ◆ 354–430
*City of God* V, 14

24.  Man is often vainglorious about his contempt of glory.‡

SAINT AUGUSTINE ◆ 354–430
*Confessions* X

25.  So passes away the glory of this world. (*Sic transit gloria mundi.*)

THOMAS À KEMPIS (THOMAS HAEMERKEN) ◆ C. 1380–1471
*Imitation of Christ* I, 3

26.  Who is there that does not voluntarily exchange health, repose, and life itself for reputation and glory, the most useless, frivolous, and false coin that passes current amongst us?

MICHEL EYQUEM DE MONTAIGNE ◆ 1533–1592
*Essays* I

---

‡  That is, both the pursuit of glory and a contempt for glory should be avoided.

27. [I]t is to God alone that glory and honor belong. And there is nothing so remote from reason as for us to go in quest of it for ourselves; for since we are indigent and necessitous within, since our essence is imperfect and continually in need of betterment, it is this betterment that we should work for.

"Of Glory," Ibid.

28. Glory consists of two parts: the one in setting too great a value upon ourselves, and the other in setting too little a value upon others.

"Of Presumption," Ibid.

29. Glory and repose are things that cannot possibly inhabit in one and the same place.

Ibid.

30. What is called vainglory is self-satisfaction, nourished by nothing but the good opinion of the multitude, so that when that is withdrawn, the satisfaction, that is to say, the chief good which every one loves, ceases. For this reason those who glory in the good opinion of the multitude anxiously and with daily care strive, labour, and struggle to preserve their fame. For the multitude is changeable and fickle, so that fame, if it be not preserved, soon passes away. As every one, moreover, is desirous to catch the praises of the people, one person will readily destroy the fame of another; and, consequently, as the object of contention is what is commonly thought to be the highest good, a great desire arises on the part of every one to keep down his fellows by every possible means, and he who at last comes off conqueror boasts more because he has

injured another person than because he has profited himself. This glory of self-satisfaction, therefore, is indeed vain, for it is really no glory.

BARUCH SPINOZA ◆ 1632–1677
*Ethics* IV, Prop. 58

# ARGUMENTS FOR THE PURSUIT OF GLORY

## BASIC ARGUMENTS

31. The glory dies not, and the grief is past.

SIR EDGERTON BRYDGES ◆ 1762–1837
*On the Death of Sir Walter Scott*

32. A man who was not impelled by any deep, instinctive feeling, to sacrifice his life for the good of others, yet was roused to such actions by a sense of glory, would by his example excite the same wish for glory....

CHARLES DARWIN ◆ 1809–1882
*Descent of Man* I, 5

33. Though God hath raised me high, yet this I count the glory of my crown: that I have reigned with your loves.

QUEEN ELIZABETH I ◆ 1533–1603
"The Golden Speech," *D'Ewes's Journal*

34. For glory gives herself only to those who have always dreamed of her.

CHARLES DE GAULLE ◆ 1890–1970
Quoted in *The New York Times,* June 1, 1958

35. I would feel deep shame before the Trojans, and
    the Trojan women with trailing garments, if like
    a coward I were to shrink aside from the fighting;
    and the spirit will not let me, since I have learned to
    be valiant and to fight always among the foremost
    ranks of the Trojans, winning for my own self great
    glory, and for my father.

    HOMER ◆ 8TH CENT. B.C.E.
    *The Iliad* VI, 441

36. Man, supposing you and I, escaping this battle, would
    be able to live on forever, ageless, immortal, so neither
    would I myself go on fighting in the foremost nor
    would I urge you into the fighting where men win
    glory. But now, seeing that the spirits of death stand
    close about us in their thousands, no man can turn
    aside nor escape them, let us go on and win glory
    for ourselves, or yield it to others.

    Ibid., XII, 322

37. They carry back bright to the coiner the mintage
    of

    man,

    The lads that will die in their glory and never be old.

    A(LFRED) E(DWARD) HOUSMAN ◆ 1859–1936
    "Bredon Hill," *A Shropshire Lad*

38. Glory is a torch to kindle the noble mind.

    SILIUS ITALICUS ◆ 25–107
    *Punica* VI

39. Glory and loveliness have pass'd away.

    JOHN KEATS ◆ 1795–1821
    Dedication to Leigh Hunt, *The Poetical Works of John Keats*

40.  Born to glory. (*Natus ad gloriam.*)

Latin Phrase

41.  We now turn away from the checkered spectacle of so much glory and so much shame.

THOMAS BABINGTON MACAULAY ✦ 1800–1859
"On Lord Bacon"

42.  Sound, sound the clarion, fill the fife,
     Throughout the sensual world proclaim,
     One crowded hour of glorious life
     Is worth an age without a name.

THOMAS OSBERT MORDAUNT ✦ 1730–1809
"The Call"

43.  It is the fortune of all good men that their virtue rises in glory after their deaths, and that the envy which evil men conceive against them never outlives them long.

PLUTARCH ✦ 46–120
*Numa Pompilius*

44.  It is the brave man's part to live with glory, or with glory die.

SOPHOCLES ✦ C. 495–406 B.C.E.
*Ajax*

## PHILOSOPHICAL ARGUMENTS

45.  [T]he better a man is, the more he is inspired by glory. The very philosophers themselves, even in

those books which they write on contempt of glory, inscribe their names.

MARCUS TULLIUS CICERO ♦ 106–43 B.C.E.
*Pro Archia*

46. There lurks in every human heart a desire of distinction, which inclines every man first to hope, and then to believe that Nature has given him something peculiar to himself.

SAMUEL JOHNSON ♦ 1709–1784
Letter to James Boswell, December 8, 1763

47. The greatest baseness of man is his seeking for glory: but even this is the greatest indication of his excellence; for, whatever possession he may have on earth, whatever health and essential comfort he may have, he is not satisfied without the esteem of men.

BLAISE PASCAL ♦ 1623–1662
*Pensées* II

# PLEASURE (PHYSICAL)

## SEX

### ARGUMENTS AGAINST THE FREE PURSUIT OF SEX*

---

#### BASIC ARGUMENTS

---

1. Beauty soon grows familiar to the lover,
   Fades in his eye, and palls upon the sense.

   > JOSEPH ADDISON ◆ 1672–1719
   > *Cato* I

2. Desire is poison at lunch and wormwood at dinner;
   your bed is a stone, friendship is hateful and your
   fancy is always fixed on one thing.

   > PIETRO ARETINO ◆ 1492–1556
   > Letter to Count di San Secondo June 24, 1537

---

\* *Arguments for* ... begin on page 143.

3. I abhor, too, the roaming lover, nor do I drink from every well; I loathe all things held in common.

CALLIMACHUS ◆ C. 300–240 B.C.E.
*Epigrams*

4. Foul lust of lechery, behold thy due. Not only dost thou darken a man's mind, But bringest destruction on his body too....

GEOFFREY CHAUCER ◆ 1343–1400
"The Man of Law's Tale," *Canterbury Tales*

5. He then joins her on her side of the bed and they engage in a back-breaking labor of love that occupies them for twenty minutes and leaves them both with a grueling headache.

JOHN CHEEVER ◆ 1912–1982
*Bullet Park*

6. I am a twentieth century failure, a happy undersexed celibate.

DENISE COFFEY ◆ 1936–
Quoted in the *News of the World*

7. Like the bee its sting, the promiscuous leave behind them in each encounter something of themselves by which they are made to suffer.

CYRIL CONNOLLY ◆ 1903–1974
*The Unquiet Grave*

8. Whoever loves, if he do not propose
The right true end of love, he's one that goes
To sea for nothing but to make him sick.

JOHN DONNE ◆ C. 1571–1631
"Love's Progress," *Elegy* 18

9. He is not a lover who does not love forever.

> EURIPIDES ◆ 485–406 B.C.E.
> *The Troades*

10. The wisest man is the likeliest to possess all worldly blessings in an eminent degree; for as that moderation which wisdom prescribes is the surest way to useful wealth, so can it alone qualify us to taste many pleasures. The wise man gratifies every appetite and every passion, while the fool sacrifices all the rest to pall and satiate one.

> HENRY FIELDING ◆ 1707–1754
> *Tom Jones* VI, 3

11. Rarely use venery but for health or offspring, never to dullness, weakness, or the injury of your own or another's peace or reputation.

> BENJAMIN FRANKLIN ◆ 1706–1790
> *The Art of Virtue*

12. "They eat him, same as a hen-spider eats a cock-spider. That's what women do—if a man lets 'em."

> STELLA GIBBONS ◆ 1902–1989
> *Cold Comfort Farm*

13. A woman takes off her claim to respect along with her garments.

> HERODOTUS ◆ C. 485–C. 425 B.C.E.
> *Histories* I, 8

14. Purely sensual love is never true or lasting....

> RICHARD VON KRAFFT-EBING ◆ 1840–1902
> *Psychopathia Sexualis* 1

15. Sensuality is the vice of young men and of old nations.

> WILLIAM E(DWARD) H(ARTPOLE) LECKY ◆ 1838–1903
> *History of European Morals*

16. There is nothing like early promiscuous sex for dispelling life's bright mysterious expectations.

> IRIS MURDOCH ◆ 1919–1999
> *A Word Child*

17. Not joy but joylessness is the mother of debauchery.

> FRIEDRICH WILHELM NIETZSCHE ◆ 1844–1900
> *Miscellaneous Maxims and Opinions* 71

18. Delight of lust is gross and brief. And weariness treads on desire.

> GAIUS PETRONIUS (PETRONIUS ARBITER) ◆ C. 27–C. 66
> In A. Baehrens, *Poetae Latinae Minores* IV, 101

19. He goeth after her straightway, as an ox goeth to the slaughter.

> *Proverbs* 7:22

20. Sensuality, too, which used to show itself coarse, smiling, unmasked, and unmistakable, is now serious, analytic, and so burdened with a sense of its responsibilities that is passes muster half the time as a new type of asceticism.

> AGNES REPPLIER ◆ 1855–1950
> *Points of View Fiction in the Pulpit*

21. Fie on sinful fantasy!
    Fie on lust and luxury!

Lust is but a bloody fire,
Kindled with unchaste desire,
Fed in heart, whose flames aspire
As thoughts do blow them, higher and higher.
Pinch him, fairies, mutually;
Pinch him for his villainy;
Pinch him, and burn him, and turn him about,
Till candles and starlight and moonshine be out.

WILLIAM SHAKESPEARE ♦ 1564–1616
*The Merry Wives of Windsor* V, v, 97

22. All this the world well knows; yet none knows well
To shun the heaven that leads men to this hell.

WILLIAM SHAKESPEARE ♦ 1564–1616
*Sonnet* 129

23. The world's books get written, its pictures painted,
its statues modelled, its symphonies composed, by
people who are free from the otherwise universal
domination of the tyranny of sex.

GEORGE BERNARD SHAW ♦ 1856–1950
"Epistle Dedicatory," *Man and Superman*

24. As concerning lust or incontinency, it is a short
pleasure, bought with long pain, a honeyed poison,
a gulf of shame, a pickpurse, a breeder of diseases,
a gall to the conscience, a corrosive to the heart,
turning man's wit into foolish madness, the body's
bane, and the soul's perdition.

JOHN TAYLOR ♦ 1578–1653
*The Unnatural Father*

25.  Let me just say, sex wasn't that great, it really wasn't.
     I mean, I thought, oh my God, this is what they've
     been trying to keep me away from?

TEENAGE MOTHER
Quoted in "Sex Education," *The Village Voice,* February 3, 1987

26.  Sex builds no roads, writes no novels, and sex certainly
     gives no meaning to anything in life but itself.

GORE VIDAL ♦ 1925–
*Rocking the Boat*

27.  Once upon a time there was an Englishman who loved
     a woman madly, hopelessly, and for many months
     he besieged the citadel and never thought to win
     it. But at last she took pity on him and murmured,
     "Yes—today. This afternoon." In the twinkling of an
     eye his face changed. "Not today," he said darkly,
     "today I am playing polo."

BARBARA WILSON ♦ 1880–1943
*The House of Memories*

## PHILOSOPHICAL ARGUMENTS

28.  The sin, then, consists not in desiring a woman, but
     in consent to the desire, and not the wish for whore-
     dom, but the consent to the wish is damnation.

PETER ABELARD (PIERRE ABEILARD) ♦ 1079–1142
*Ethics*

29.  Lust requires for its consummation darkness and
     secrecy; and this not only when unlawful inter-
     course is desired, but even such fornication as the

earthly city has legalized. Where there is no fear of punishment, these permitted pleasures still shrink from the public eye.

SAINT AUGUSTINE ◆ 354–430
*City of God* XVIII

30. I came to Carthage, where a cauldron of illicit loves leapt and boiled about me. I was not yet in love, but I was in love with love.... My longing then was to love and to be loved, but most when I obtained the enjoyment of the body of the person who loved me. Thus I polluted the stream of friendship with the filth of unclean desire and sullied its limpidity with the hell of lust. And vile and unclean as I was, so great was my vanity that I was bent upon passing for clean and courtly. And I did fall in love, simply from wanting to. O my God, 'my Mercy, with how much bitterness didst Thou in Thy goodness sprinkle the delights of that time! I was loved, and our love came to the bond of consummation: I wore my chains with bliss but with torment too, for I was scourged with red hot rods of jealousy, with suspicions and fears and tempers and quarrels.

SAINT AUGUSTINE ◆ 354–430
*Confessions* III, 1

31. I in my great worthlessness—for it was greater thus early—had begged You for chastity, saying "Grant me chastity and continence, but not yet." For I was afraid that You would hear my prayer too soon, and too soon would heal me from the disease of lust which I wanted satisfied rather than extinguished.

*Ibid.,* VIII, 7

32. Lust is an appetite of the mind by which temporal goods are preferred to eternal goods.

> SAINT AUGUSTINE ◆ 354–430
> "On Lying"

33. Of bodily pleasure I can think of little to say. Its pursuit is full of anxiety and its fulfillment full of remorse. Frequently, like a kind of reward for wickedness, it causes great illness and unbearable pain for those who make it their source of enjoyment. I do not know what happiness lies in its passions, but that the end of pleasure is sorrow is known to everyone who cares to recall his own excesses.

> (ANICUS MANLIUS SEVERINUS) BOETHIUS ◆ C. 480–524
> *The Consolation of Philosophy* III, 7

34. From sensuousness arises sorrow and from sensuousness arises fear. If a man is free from sensuousness, he is free from fear and sorrow. From lust arises sorrow and from lust arises fear. If a man is free from lust, he is free from fear and sorrow.

> BUDDHA (SIDDHARTHA GAUTAMA) ◆ C. 563–483 B.C.E.
> *The Dhammapada* 16.66

35. The Master said, In vain have I looked for one whose desire to build up his moral power was as strong as his sexual desire.

> CONFUCIUS ◆ 551–479 B.C.E.
> *Analects* IX, 4

36. As regards sexual matters, you should remain pure, so far as you can, before marriage, and, if you indulge, let it be lawfully. But do not therefore become

aggravating or censorious to those who do indulge, nor frequently boast that you yourself do not.

EPICTETUS ✦ C. 55–135
*The Handbook of Epictetus* 33

37. You tell me that the stimulus of the flesh makes you too prone to the pleasures of love. Provided that you do not break the laws or good customs and do not distress any of your neighbours or do harm to your body or squander your pittance, you may indulge your inclination as you please. Yet it is impossible not to come up against one or other of these barriers: for the pleasures of love never profited a man and he is lucky if they do him no harm.

EPICURUS ✦ 341–270 B.C.E.
*Vatican Sayings* LI

38. The first measure of security is to watch over one's youth and to guard against what makes havoc of all by means of pestering desires.

Ibid., LXXX

39. It is indeed one of the most important social tasks of education to restrain, confine, and subject to an individual control (itself identical with the demands of society) the sexual instinct when it breaks forth in the form of the reproductive function. In its own interests, accordingly, society would postpone the child's full development until it has attained a certain stage of intellectual maturity, since educability practically ceases with the full onset of the sexual instinct. Without this the instinct would break all bounds, and the laboriously erected structure of civilization would be swept away. Nor is the task of

restraining it ever an easy one; success in this direction is often poor and, sometimes, only too great.
At bottom society's motive is economic; since it has
not means enough to support life for its members
without work on their part, it must see to it that the
number of these members is restricted and their
energies directed away from sexual activities on
to their work—the eternal primordial struggle for
existence, therefore, persisting to the present day.

SIGMUND FREUD ◆ 1856–1939
General Introduction to *Psycho-Analysis*

40.  For all that is in the world, the lust of the flesh, and
the lust of the eyes, and the pride of life, is not of the
Father, but is of the world. And the world passeth
away, and the lust thereof: but he that doeth the will
of God abideth for ever.

SAINT JOHN ◆ 1ST CENTURY
*1 John* 2:15-17

41.  For the flesh lusteth against the Spirit, and the Spirit
against the flesh: and these are contrary the one to the
other: so that ye cannot do the things that ye would.

SAINT PAUL ◆ 1ST CENTURY
*Galatians* 5:17

42.  Abstain from fleshly lusts, which war against the
soul.

SAINT PETER ◆ 1ST CENTURY
*1 Peter* 2:11

43. Now everyone recognizes that the emotional state for which we make this "Love" responsible rises in souls aspiring to be knit in the closest union with some beautiful object, and that this aspiration takes two different forms, that of the good whose devotion is for beauty itself, and that other which seeks its consummation in some vile act. Those who love beauty of person without carnal desire love for beauty's sake; those that have—for women, of course—the copulative love, have the further purpose of self-perpetuation: as long as they are led by these motives, both are on the right path, though the first have taken the nobler way.

> PLOTINUS ◆ 205–270
> *Ennead III,* fifth tractate

44. If…one considers the important part which the sexual impulse in all its degrees and nuances plays not only on the stage and in novels, but also in the real world, where, next to the love of life, it shows itself the strongest and most powerful of motives, constantly lays claim to half the powers and thoughts of the younger portion of mankind, is the ultimate goal of almost all human effort, exerts an adverse influence on the most important events, interrupts the most serious occupations every hour, sometimes embarrasses for a while even the greatest minds, does not hesitate to intrude with its trash interfering with the negotiations of statesmen and the investigations of men of learning, knows how to slip its love letters and locks of hair even into ministerial portfolios and philosophical manuscripts, and no less devises daily the most entangled and the worst actions, destroys the most valuable relationships, breaks the firmest bonds, demands the sacrifice some-

times of life or health, sometimes of wealth, rank, and happiness, nay, robs those who are otherwise honest of all conscience, makes those who have hitherto been faithful, traitors; accordingly, on the whole, appears as a malevolent demon that strives to pervert, confuse, and overthrow everything; then one will be forced to cry, Wherefore all this noise?

ARTHUR SCHOPENHAUER ♦ 1788–1860
*The World as Will and Idea*

45. Every lover, after the ultimate consummation of the great work, finds himself cheated; for the illusion has vanished by means of which the individual was here the dupe of the species.

Ibid.

46. In the friendship of the lover there is no real kindness; he has an appetite and wants to feed upon you. "Just as the wolf loves the lamb, so the lover adores his beloved."

SOCRATES ♦ C. 428–348 B.C.E.
Quoted in Plato, *Phaedrus*

47. The love of a harlot, that is to say, the lust of sexual intercourse, which arouses from mere external form, and absolutely all love which recognizes any other cause than the freedom of the mind, easily passes into hatred, unless, which is worse, it becomes a species of delirium, and thereby discord is cherished rather than concord.

BARUCH SPINOZA ♦ 1632–1677
*Ethics* 111, 29

## THE SPECIAL CASE OF ADULTERY

48. Passion is the evil in adultery. If a man has no opportunity of living with another man's wife, but if it is obvious for some reason that he would like to do so, and would do so if he could, he is no less guilty than if he was caught in the act.

> SAINT AUGUSTINE ◆ 354–430
> *The Problem of Free Choice*

49. Four things happen to the thoughtless man who takes another man's wife: he lowers himself, his pleasure is restless, he is blamed by others, he goes to hell. Yes. The degradation of the soul, a frightened pleasure, the danger of the law, the path of hell. Considering these four, let not a man go after another man's wife.

> BUDDHA (SIDDHARTHA GAUTAMA) ◆ C. 563–483 B.C.E.
> *The Dhammapada* 22.79

50. And she [Potiphar's wife] caught him by his garment, saying, Lie with me: and he left his garment in her hand, and fled, and got him out.

> *Genesis* 39:12

51. Lust not after her beauty in thine heart; neither let her take thee with her eyelids. Can a man take fire in his bosom, and his clothes not be burned? Can one go upon hot coals, and his feet not be burned? So he that goeth in to his neighbor's wife; whosoever toucheth her shall not be innocent.

> *Proverbs* 6:25, 27-29

52. "She told me a good deal about Mr. Driver," said Jane. "About his wife and other things."

    "Ah, the other things," said Miss Doggett obscurely. "Of course, we never saw anything of those. We knew that it went on, of course—in London, I believe."

    "Yes, it seems suitable that things like that should go on in London," Jane agreed.

    BARBARA PYM ◆ 1913–1980
    *Jane and Prudence*

53. When daisies pied and violets blue
    And lady-smocks all silver-white
    And cuckoo-buds of yellow hue
    Do paint the meadows with delight,
    The cuckoo then, on every tree,
    Mocks married men; for thus sings he,
    Cuckoo; Cuckoo, cuckoo;
    O, word of fear,
    Unpleasing to a married ear!

    WILLIAM SHAKESPEARE ◆ 1564–1616
    *Love's Labour's Lost* V, i, 902

# ARGUMENTS FOR THE FREE (OR FAIRLY FREE) PURSUIT OF SEX

## BASIC ARGUMENTS

54. It isn't that I was what's called, rather unhandsomely, "highly sexed." But it was such a surprise that one could attract. It was like a stream finding out that it could still move a rock. The pleasure of one's effect on

other people still exists in age—what's called making a hit. But the hit is much rarer and made of different stuff.

ENID BAGNOLD ◆ 1889–1981
*Autobiography*

55. Many [Italian men] are disposed to make love at the drop of a hat, anywhere, in a car, on a beach, behind a bush, on mountain summits, under water, or even in a bed, during the day or at night.

LUIGI BARZINI ◆ 1908–1984
*The Italians*

56. Variety is the soul of pleasure.

APHRA BEHN ◆ 1640–1689
*The Rover*

57. Love is a delightful day's journey. At the farther end kiss your companion and say farewell.

AMBROSE BIERCE ◆ 1842–1914
*Collected Works* VIII

58. Abstinence sows sand all over
The ruddy limbs and flaming hair,
But Desire gratified
Plants fruits of life and beauty there.

WILLIAM BLAKE ◆ 1757–1827
*Ms. Notebooks*

59. Everything that lives is holy....
The lust of the goat is the glory of God.

WILLIAM BLAKE ◆ 1757–1827
*The Marriage of Heaven and Hell*

60.  That delicious passion, in spite of acid disappointment, gin-house prudence and book worm philosophy, I hold to be the first of human joys, our dearest blessing here below.

ROBERT BURNS ♦ 1759–1796
Autobiographical memorandum prepared for
Dr. John Moore, August 1787

61.  Julia's voice was lost, except in sighs,
Until too late for useful conversation;
The tears were gushing from her gentle eyes,
I wish, indeed, they had not had occasion,
But who, alas! can love, and then be wise?
Not that remorse did not oppose temptation;
A little still she strove, and much repented,
And whispering "I will ne'er consent" consented.

GEORGE NOEL GORDON, LORD BYRON ♦ 1788–1824
*Don Juan* 1.117

62.  In her first passion woman loves her lover,
In all the others all she loves is love.

Ibid., 3.1

63.  Lovers may be, and, indeed, generally are enemies, but they never can be friends.

GEORGE NOEL GORDON, LORD BYRON ♦ 1788–1824
Letter to Lady _____, November 10, 1822

64.  I look upon love as a sort of hostile transaction, very necessary to keep the world going, but by no means a sinecure to the parties concerned.

Ibid.

65. But what a woman says to her lusting lover it is best to write in wind and swift-flowing water.

GAIUS VALERIUS CATULLUS ♦ 87–54 B.C.E.
*Carmina* lxx

66. Dined with the Lady Willingdon (7 December, 1942). Emerald (Cunard) was 45 minutes late, as she so often and irritatingly is. At one point Emerald, with mischief in her old, over-made up eyes, declared that no man was faithful to his wife for more than three years. "That," she added, "is a biological fact." "You can never have known my Freeman," Lady Willing-don retorted. "'Perhaps better than you think," was Emerald's reply.

HENRY "CHIPS" CHANNON ♦ 1897–1958
*Diaries*

67. If our elaborate and dominating bodies are given us to be denied at every turn, if our nature is always wrong and wicked, how ineffectual we are—like fishes not meant to swim.

CYRIL CONNOLLY ♦ 1903–1974
*The Unquiet Grave*

68. It is the fear of middle-age in the young, of old-age in the middle-aged, which is the prime cause of infidelity, that infallible rejuvenator.

Ibid.

69. Sweet dalliance keepeth wrinkles long away;
Repentance follows them that have refused.

HENRY CONSTABLE ♦ 1562–1613
*Sonnets to Diana*

70. The law of battle for the possession of the female appears to prevail throughout the whole great class of mammals.

> CHARLES DARWIN ◆ 1809–1882
> *Descent of Man* II, 18

71. Chastity is the most unnatural of the sexual perversions.

> REMY DE GOURMONT ◆ 1858–1915
> *Promenades philosophiques*

72. Pushkin, the poet of women's feet, sung of their feet in his verse. Others don't sing their praises, but they can't look at their feet without a thrill—and it's not only their feet.

> FYODOR MIKHAILOVICH DOSTOEVSKY ◆ 1821–1881
> *The Brothers Karamazov*

73. 'Tis good to be off wi' the old love
    Before you are on wi' the new.

> RICHARD EDWARDS ◆ 1523–1566
> *Damon and Pithias*

74. Sexual pleasure, widely used and not abused, may prove the stimulus and liberation of our finest and most exalted activities.

> HAVELOCK ELLIS ◆ 1859–1939
> *Impressions and Comments*

75. A woman can look both moral and exciting—if she also looks as if it was quite a struggle.

> EDNA FERBER ◆ 1887–1968
> Quoted in *Reader's Digest,* December 1954

76. What is commonly called love, namely the desire of satisfying a voracious appetite with a certain quantity of delicate white human flesh.

HENRY FIELDING ◆ 1707–1754
*Tom Jones* ii, 9

77. Love is like linen—often changed, the sweeter.

PHINEAS FLETCHER ◆ 1582–1650
*Sicelides* III

78. Retrospectively I would agree with Luis Bunuel that sex without sin is like an egg without salt.

CARLOS FUENTES ◆ 1928–
"How I Started to Write," in *The Art of the Personal*, ed. Phillip Lopate

79. Variety's the source of joy below, From whence still fresh revolving pleasures flow. In books and love, the mind one end pursues, And only change th' expiring flame renews.

JOHN GAY ◆ 1685–1732
*On a Miscellany of Poems*

80. With the venerable proconsul [Gordianus], his son, who had accompanied him into Africa as his lieuten-ant, was likewise declared emperor. His manners were less pure, but his character was equally amiable with that of his father. Twenty two acknowledged concubines, and a library of sixty-two thousand volumes, attested the variety of his inclinations, and from the productions which he left behind him, it appears that the former as well as the latter were designed for use rather than ostentation.

EDWARD GIBBON ◆ 1737–1794
*Decline and Fall of the Roman Empire* VII

81. Although the progress of civilisation has undoubtedly contributed to assuage the fiercer passions of human nature, it seems to have been less favourable to the virtue of chastity, whose most dangerous enemy is the softness of the mind. The refinements of life corrupt while they polish the intercourse of the sexes. The gross appetite of love becomes most dangerous when it is elevated, or rather, indeed, disguised by sentimental passion.The elegance of dress, of motion, and of manners gives a lustre to beauty, and inflames the senses through the imagination. Luxurious entertainments, midnight dances, and licentious spectacles, present at once temptations and opportunity to female frailty.

Ibid., IX

82. The laws of Constantine against rapes were dictated with very little indulgence for the most amiable weaknesses of human nature; since the description of that crime was applied not only to the brutal violence which compelled, but even to the gentle seduction which might persuade, an unmarried woman, under the age of twenty-five, to leave the house of her parents.

Ibid., XIV

83. How much more sensuality invites to art than does sentimentality.

ANDRÉ GIDE ◆ 1869–1951
*Journals* 1912

84. To win a woman in the first place one must please her, then undress her, and then somehow get her

clothes back on her. Finally, so that she will allow you to leave her, you've got to annoy her.

JEAN GIRAUDOUX ◆ 1882–1944
*Amphitryon* 38 I

85.  My life with girls has ended, though till lately I was up to it and soldiered on not ingloriously; now on this wall will hang my weapons and my lyre, discharged from the war.

HORACE (QUINTUS HORATIUS) ◆ 65–8 B.C.E.
*Odes* III, xxvi, 1

86.  Sex is the salt of life.

JAMES GIBBONS HUNEKER ◆ 1860–1921
*Painted Veils*

87.  And there are, of course, many people who are genuinely repelled by the simplest and most natural stirrings of sexual feeling. But these people are perverts who have fallen into hatred of their fellow man: thwarted, disappointed, unfulfilled people, of whom, alas, our civilization contains so many.

D(AVID) H(ERBERT) LAWRENCE ◆ 1885–1930
*Pornography and Obscenity*

88.  If a woman hasn't got a tiny streak of harlot in her, she's a dry stick as a rule.

Ibid.

89.  Girls who put out are tramps. Girls who don't are ladies. This is, however, a rather archaic usage of the word. Should one of you boys happen upon a girl

who doesn't put out, do not jump to the conclusion that you have found a lady. What you have probably found is a lesbian.

FRAN LEBOWITZ ♦ 1950–
*Metropolitan Life*

90. Had we but world enough, and time,
This coyness, lady, were no crime.

ANDREW MARVELL ♦ 1621–1678
*To His Coy Mistress*

91. The spirit is often most free when the body is satiated with pleasure; indeed, sometimes the stars shine more brightly seen from the gutter than from the hilltop.

W(ILLIAM) SOMERSET MAUGHAM ♦ 1874–1965
*The Summing Up*

92. Women can always be caught; that's the first rule of the game.

OVID (PUBLIUS OVIDIUS NASO) ♦ 43 B.C.E.– C. 18
*The Art of Love* 1

93. Desire is indeed powerful; it engenders belief.

MARCEL PROUST ♦ 1871–1922
*The Sweet Cheat Gone* VI

94. Love and eggs are best when they are fresh.

*Russian Proverb*

95. Morality in sexual relations, when it is free from superstition, consists essentially of respect for the

other person, and unwillingness to use that person solely as a means of personal gratification, without regard to his or her desires.

BERTRAND RUSSELL ◆ 1872–1970
*Marriage and Morals* XI

96. It is as unjust to possess a woman exclusively as to possess slaves.

MARQUIS DE SADE ◆ 1740–1814
*La Philosophie dans le boudoir*

97. A young man married is a man that's marred....

WILLIAM SHAKESPEARE ◆ 1564–1616
*All's Well That Ends Well* II, iii

98. The primrose path of dalliance....

WILLIAM SHAKESPEARE ◆ 1564–1616
*Hamlet* I, iii

99. Love is free; to promise for ever to love the same woman is not less absurd than to promise to believe that same creed; such a vow in both cases excludes us from all inquiry.

PERCY BYSSHE SHELLEY ◆ 1792–1822
Notes to *Queen Mab*

100. Love withers under constraint: its very essence is liberty: it is compatible neither with obedience, jealousy, nor fear....

Ibid.

101. I think, till thirty, or with some a little longer, People should dress in a way that is most likely to procure the love of the opposite sex.

WILLIAM SHENSTONE ◆ 1714–1763
"On Dress"

102. Alas, I know he is the hermaphrodite whose love looks up through the appletree with a golden indeterminate face. While we drive along the road in the evening, talking as impersonally as a radio discussion, he tells me, "A boy with green eyes and long lashes, whom I had never seen before, took me into the back of a printshop and made love to me, and for two weeks I went around remembering the numbers on bus conductors' hats."

"One should love beings whatever their sex," I reply, but withdraw into the dark with my obstreperous shape of shame, offended with my own flesh which cannot metamorphose into a printshop boy with armpits like chalices.

ELIZABETH SMART ◆ 1913–1986
*By Grand Central Station I Sat Down and Wept*

103. [I]t is no mere accident (as Orwell knew) that the standardization of sexual life, either through controlled license or compelled puritanism, should accompany totalitarian politics.

GEORGE STEINER ◆ 1929–
*Language and Silence*

104. A wise woman should never give herself for the first time by appointment—it should be an unforeseen delight.

STENDHAL (MARIE HENRI BEYLE) ◆ 1783–1842
*On Love*

105. Man is not free to refuse to do the thing which gives him more pleasure than any other conceivable action.

Ibid.

106. I could walk with Jack [John F. Kennedy] into a room full of a hundred women,…and at least eighty-five of them would be willing to sacrifice their honor and everything else if they could get into a pad with him.

FRANK THOMPSON, JR. ◆ 1918–1989
Quoted in Doris Goodwin, *The Fitzgeralds and the Kennedys*

107. To say that you can love one person all your life is just like saying that one candle will continue burning as long as you live.

LEO NIKOLAEVICH TOLSTOY ◆ 1828–1910
*The Kreutzer Sonata*

108. Of the delights of this world man cares most for sexual intercourse. He will go any length for it—risk fortune, character, reputation, life itself. And what do you think he has done? In a thousand years you would never guess—He has left it out of his heaven! Prayer takes its place.

MARK TWAIN (SAMUEL LANGHORNE CLEMENS) ◆ 1835–1910
*Notebook*

109. I believe in the flesh and the appetites;
Seeing, hearing, feeling, are miracles, and each
part and tag of me is a miracle.

WALT WHITMAN ◆ 1819–1892
"Song of Myself," *Leaves of Grass*

110. Young men want to be faithful, and are not; old men want to be faithless, and cannot.

> OSCAR (FINGALL O'FLAHERTIE WILLS) WILDE ♦ 1854–1900
> *The Picture of Dorian Gray*

111. Those who are faithful know only the trivial side of love; it is the faithless who know love's tragedies.

> Ibid.

112. The only difference between a caprice and a life-long passion is that the caprice lasts a little longer.

> Ibid.

113. When a man has once loved a woman he will do anything for her except continue to love her.

> OSCAR (FINGALL O'FLAHERTIE WILLS) WILDE ♦ 1854–1900
> *An Ideal Husband*

114. Devils can be driven out of the heart by the touch of a hand on a hand, or a mouth on a mouth.

> TENNESSEE (THOMAS LANIER) WILLIAMS ♦ 1914–1983
> *The Milk Train Doesn't Stop Here Anymore*

---

## PHILOSOPHICAL ARGUMENTS

---

115. Much of our most highly valued cultured heritage has been acquired at the cost of our sexuality.

> SIGMUND FREUD ♦ 1856–1939
> *An Outline of Psychoanalysis*

116.  The woman who goes to bed with a man should put off her modesty with her skirt and put it on again with her petticoat.

> MICHEL EYQUEM DE MONTAIGNE ◆ 1533–1592
> "Power of the Imagination," *Essays* I, 21

117.  [I]t is a wonderful sign of our defectiveness that acquaintance and familiarity disgust us with one another.

> "Apology for Raymond Sebond," Ibid., II, 12

118.  Love is nothing save an insatiate thirst to enjoy a greedily desired object.

> Ibid., III

119.  The truth is that it is contrary to the nature of love if it is not violent, and contrary to the nature of violence if it is constant. And those who are astonished at this and exclaim against it and seek out the causes of this malady in women as if it were unnatural and incredible, why don't they see how often they accept it in themselves without being appalled and calling it a miracle? It would perhaps be more strange to see any stability in it. It is not simply a bodily passion. If there is no end to avarice and ambition, neither is there any to lechery. It still lives after satiety; no constant satisfaction or end can be prescribed to it, for it always goes beyond its possession.

> "On Some Verses of Virgil," Ibid., III, 5

120. Christianity gave Eros poison to drink: he did not die of it but degenerated—into a vice.

> FRIEDRICH WILHELM NIETZSCHE ◆ 1844–1900
> *Beyond Good and Evil* IV, 168

121. Violent pleasures which reach the soul through the body are generally of this sort—they are reliefs of pain.

> PLATO ◆ C. 428–348 B.C.E.
> *The Republic* 9

122. There is no use arguing about polygamy; it must be taken as *de facto* existing everywhere, and the only question is how it will be regulated.

> ARTHUR SCHOPENHAUER ◆ 1788–1860
> *The World as Will and Idea*

123. We all live, at any rate for a time, and most of us always, in polygamy. And so, since every man needs many women, there is nothing fairer than to allow him, nay, to make it incumbent upon him, to provide for many women.

> Ibid.

---

## THE SPECIAL CASE OF ADULTERY

---

124. There is not a man in the world who doth not look at another's wife, if beautiful and young, with a degree of desire.

> *Hitopadesa ("Book of Good Counsels"):*
> *Fables and Proverbs from the Sanscrit* ◆ *c. 500*

125. Adultery is the application of democracy to love.

> H(ENRY) L(OUIS) MENCKEN ◆ 1880–1956
> *A Book of Burlesques Sententiae*

126. 'Tis sweet to think, that, where'er we rove,
     We are sure to find something blissful and dear,
     And that, when we're far from the lips we love,
     We've but to make love to the lips we are near.

> THOMAS MOORE ◆ 1779–1852
> " 'Tis Sweet to Think," *Irish Melodies*

127. "Isn't it nice the way the French take it for granted
     one isn't married and never ask for the girl's passport
     for the *fiches*?" she said, in their room....

> VENETIA MURRAY ◆ 1932–
> *The Twelve Days of Christmas*

128. And it came to pass in an eveningtide, that David
     arose from off his bed, and walked upon the roof of
     the king's house: and from the roof he saw a woman
     washing herself; and the woman was very beautiful
     to look upon. And David sent and enquired after
     the woman. And one said, Is not this Bath-sheba,
     the daughter of Eliam, the wife of Uriah the Hittite?
     And David sent messengers, and took her; and she
     came in unto him, and he lay with her....

> *2 Samuel* 11:2-4

129. Thou shalt not die. Die for adultery!
     No: The wren goes fo't, and the small gilded fly
     Does lecher in my sight.
     Let copulation thrive; for Gloucester's bastard son

Was kinder to his father than my daughters
Got 'tween the lawful sheets.

WILLIAM SHAKESPEARE ◆ 1564–1616
*King Lear* IV, vi, 108

130. No man worth having is true to his wife, or can be true to his wife, or ever was, or ever will be so.

JOHN VANBRUGH ◆ 1664–1726
*The Relapse*

131. In matters of love a woman's oath is no more to be minded than a man's.

Ibid.

132. Adultery is an evil only inasmuch as it is a theft; but we do not steal that which is given to us.

VOLTAIRE (FRANÇOIS MARIE AROUET) ◆ 1694–1778
"Adultery," *Philosophical Dictionary*

# DRINK

## ARGUMENTS AGAINST THE FREE PURSUIT OF DRINK (OR SIMILAR PLEASURES)*

### BASIC ARGUMENTS

133. One reason I don't drink is that I want to know when I am having a good time.

> NANCY ASTOR ◆ 1879–1964
> Quoted in *Reader's Digest,* 1960

134. For when the wine is in, the wit is out.

> THOMAS BECON ◆ 1512–1567
> *Catechism* 375

135. The wine urges me on, the bewitching wine, which sets even a wise man to singing and to laughing gently and rouses him up to dance and brings forth words which were better unspoken.

> HOMER ◆ 8TH CENT. B.C.E.
> *The Odyssey* XIV, 1. 463

---

* *Arguments for . . .* begin on page 163.

136. A drunken man staggereth in his vomit.

*Isaiah* 19:14

137. Even though a number of people have tried, no one has found a way to drink for a living.

JEAN KERR ◆ 1923–2003
*Poor Richard*

138. Long quaffing maketh a short life.

JOHN LYLY ◆ C. 1554–1606
*Euphues: The Anatomy of Wit*

139. Philip Toynbee had an unfortunate disposition to collapse under drink as though a sniper had picked him off.

JESSICA MITFORD ◆ 1917–1996
*The Face of Philip*

140. [W]hile the abolition of American slavery was numerically first, the abolition of the liquor traffic is not morally second.

ELIZABETH STUART PHELPS ◆ 1844–1911
*Chapters from a Life*

141. Alcohol is a good preservative for everything but brains.

MARY PETTIBONE POOLE ◆ C. 1938
*A Glass Eye at a Keyhole*

142. Look not thou upon the wine when it is red, when it giveth his color in the cup, when it moveth itself

aright. At the last it biteth like a serpent, and stingeth like an adder.

*Proverbs* 23:31-32

143. If a man be discreet enough to take to hard drinking in his youth, before his general emptiness is ascertained, his friends invariably credit him with a host of shining qualities which, we are given to understand, lie balked and frustrated by his one unfortunate weakness.

AGNES REPPLIER ◆ 1855-1950
*Points of View*

144. Drunkenness doesn't create vices, but it brings them to the fore.

SENECA THE YOUNGER (LUCIUS ANNAEUS
SENECA) ◆ C. 4 B.C.E.-54
*Letters to Lucilius* 83.20

145. It [alcohol] provokes the desire, but it takes away the performance.

WILLIAM SHAKESPEARE ◆ 1564-1616
*Macbeth* II, iii, 34

146. O God! that men should put an enemy in their mouths to steal away their brains; that we should, with joy, pleasance, revel, and applause, transform ourselves into beasts.

WILLIAM SHAKESPEARE ◆ 1564-1616
*Othello* II, iii, 293

147.  Unrecognized alcoholism is the ruling pathology among writers and intellectuals.

DIANA TRILLING ◆ 1905–1996
Quoted in *The New York Times Book Review,* October 3, 1993

---

## PHILOSOPHICAL ARGUMENTS

---

148.  The variety of behavior in men that have drunk too much is the same with that of madmen: some of them being raging, others loving, others laughing, all extravagantly, but according to their several domineering passions.

THOMAS HOBBES ◆ 1588–1679
*Leviathan* VIII

149.  That which the sober man keeps in his breast the drunken man lets out at the lips. Astute people, when they want to ascertain a man's true character, make him drunk.

MARTIN LUTHER ◆ 1483–1546
*Table Talk* DCXCIX

150.  An old man is twice a child, and so is a drunken man.

PLATO ◆ C. 428–348 B.C.E.
*Laws* I

# ARGUMENTS FOR THE FREE PURSUIT OF DRINK

151. If all be true that I do think,
There are five reasons we should drink;
Good wine—a friend—or being dry—
Or lest we should be by and by—
Or any other reason why.

DEAN ALDRICH ◆ 1647–1710
*Reasons for Drinking*

152. Drink wine, drink poetry, drink virtue, drink as you wish.

CHARLES BAUDELAIRE ◆ 1821–1867
*Le Spleen de Paris*

153. Man, being reasonable, must get drunk;
The best of Life is but intoxication.

GEORGE NOEL GORDON, LORD BYRON ◆ 1788–1824
*Don Juan* 2.179

154. A very merry, dancing, drinking,
Laughing, quaffing, and unthinking time.

JOHN DRYDEN ◆ 1631–1700
*Secular Mosque* 1.39

155. A man hath no better thing under the sun, than to eat, and to drink, and to be merry.

*Ecclesiastes* 8:15

156. Today it is our pleasure to be drunk.

> HENRY FIELDING ♦ 1707–1754
> *Tom Thumb*

157. Better be jocund with the fruitful Grape
Than sadden after none, or bitter, Fruit.

> EDWARD FITZGERALD ♦ 1809–1883
> *The Rubáiyát of Omar Khayyam*

158. Ah, my Beloved, fill the Cup that clears
To-Day of past Regret and future Fears:
To-morrow!—Why, To-morrow I may be
Myself with Yesterday's Sev'n thousand Years.

> Ibid.

159. I wonder often what the Vintners buy
One half so precious as the stuff they sell.

> Ibid.

160. Drink! For you know not whence you came, nor why:
Drink! For you know not why you go, nor where.

> Ibid.

161. Best while you have it use your breath,
There is no drinking after death.

> JOHN FLETCHER ♦ 1579–1625
> *The Bloody Brother*

162. I fear the man who drinks water
And so remembers this morning what the rest of
us said last night.

> Greek Anthology ♦ c. 700 B.C.E.–c. 900

163. No poems can please for long or live that are written by water-drinkers.

HORACE (QUINTUS HORATIUS) ◆ 65–8 B.C.E.
*Epistles* I, xix, 1. 2

164. Now for drinks, now for some dancing with a good beat.

HORACE (QUINTUS HORATIUS) ◆ 65–8 B.C.E.
*Odes* I, xxxvii, 1

165. Let us eat and drink; for tomorrow we shall die.

*Isaiah* 22:13

166. A man who exposes himself when he is intoxicated, has not the art of getting drunk.

SAMUEL JOHNSON ◆ 1709–1784
Quoted in Boswell, *Life of Johnson*, April 24, 1779

167. I've a head like a concertina,
I've a tongue like a button-stick,
I've a mouth like an old potato,
and I'm more than a little sick,
But I've had my fun o' the Corp'ral's Guard;
I've made the cinders fly,
And I'm here in the Clink for a thundering drink
and blacking the Corporal's eye.

RUDYARD KIPLING ◆ 1865–1936
*Cells*

168. One more drink and I'd have been under the host.

DOROTHY PARKER ◆ 1893–1967
Quoted in Howard Teichmann, *George S. Kaufman*

169.  In wine there is truth. (*In vino veritas.*)

> PLINY THE ELDER (GAIUS PLINIUS SECUNDUS) ♦ 23–79
> *Natural History* 14.141

170.  There are more old drunkards than old doctors.

> *French Proverb*

171.  Over the bottle many a friend is found.

> *Yiddish Proverb*

172.  Give strong drink unto him that is ready to perish, and wine unto those that be of heavy hearts. Let him drink, and forget his poverty, and remember his misery no more.

> *Proverbs* 31:4

173.  Thou knowest in the state of innocency Adam fell; and what should poor Jack Falstaff do in the days of villany. Thou seest I have more flesh than another man, and therefore more frailty.

> WILLIAM SHAKESPEARE ♦ 1564–1616
> *King Henry IV Part 1*, III, iii, 184

174.  A bumper of good liquor
      Will end a contest quicker
      Than justice, judge, or vicar.

> RICHARD BRINSLEY SHERIDAN ♦ 1751–1816
> *The Duenna* 2.3

175.  I liked the taste of beer, its live, white lather, its brass-bright depths, the sudden world through the

wet-brown walls of the glass, the tilted rush to the lips and the slow swallowing down to the lapping belly, the salt on the tongue, the foam at the corners.

DYLAN THOMAS ◆ 1914–1953
*Portrait of the Artist as a Young Dog*

# MISCELLANY

## ARGUMENTS AGAINST THE PURSUIT OF WEALTH AND POWER

1. They [Americans] must win gold, predominance, power; crush rivals, subdue nature. They have their hearts set on the means and never...think of the end....They are eager, restless, positive, because they are superficial. To what end all this stir, noise, greed, struggle?

    HENRI FREDERIC AMIEL ◆ 1821–1881
    *Journal*

2. It is because you don't know the end and purpose of things that you think the wicked and the criminal have power and happiness.

    (ANICUS MANLIUS SEVERINUS) BOETHIUS ◆ C. 480–524
    *The Consolation of Philosophy* I, vi

3. Riches are unable to quench insatiable greed; power does not make a man master of himself if he is imprisoned by the indissoluble chains of wicked lusts;

and when high office is bestowed on unworthy men, so far from making them worthy, it only betrays them and reveals their unworthiness.

*Ibid., II, vi*

4. He who for himself or others craves not for sons or power or wealth, who puts not his own success before the success of righteousness, he is virtuous, and righteous, and wise.

BUDDHA (SIDDHARTHA GAUTAMA) ◆ C. 563–483 B.C.E.
*The Dhammapada* 6.47

5. If happiness hae not her seat
   And centre in the breast,
   We may be wise, or rich, or great,
   But never can be blest.

ROBERT BURNS ◆ 1759–1796
*Epistle to Davie*

6. It is difficult to generalize why so many Latino/as moved toward conservative...views....For many, I believe it is basically a matter of desiring material acquisitions. It is difficult to maintain a collective ideology in a society where possessions and power-status equal self-worth.

ANA CASTILLO ◆ 1953–
*Massacre of the Dreamers*

7. The happy and blessed state belongs not to abundance of riches or dignity of position or any office or power, but to freedom from pain and moderation

in feelings and an attitude of mind which imposes the limits ordained by nature.

EPICURUS ◆ 341–270 B.C.E.
*Fragments* 85

8.   Envy is the adversary of the fortunate.

EPICTETUS ◆ C. 55–135
*Encheiridion*

9.   The man who blames providence because the wicked are not punished, but are strong and rich, is doing much the same as if, when they had lost their eyes, he said that they had not been punished because their nails were sound.

EPICTETUS ◆ C. 55–135
*Fragments* 13

10.   Human felicity is produced not so much by great pieces of good fortune that seldom happen, as by little advantages that occur every day.

BENJAMIN FRANKLIN ◆ 1706–1790
*Autobiography*

11.   A certain man made a great supper, and bade many: And sent his servant at supper time to say to them that were bidden, Come; for all things are now ready. And they all with one consent began to make excuse. The first said unto him, I have bought a piece of ground, and I must needs go and see it: I pray thee have me excused. And another said, I have bought five yoke of oxen, and I go to prove them: I pray thee have me excused. And another said, I have married

a wife, and therefore I cannot come. So that servant came, and shewed his lord these things. Then the master of the house being angry said to his servant, Go out quickly into the streets and lanes of the city, and bring in hither the poor, and the maimed, and the halt, and the blind. And the servant said, Lord, it is done as thou hast commanded, and yet there is room. And the lord said unto the servant, Go out into the highways and hedges, and compel them to come in, that my house may be filled. For I say unto you, That none of those men which were bidden shall taste of my supper.

JESUS ◆ C. 4 B.C.E.–30
*Luke* 14:16-24

12. If on the sudden he begins to rise:
No man that lives can count his enemies.

THOMAS MIDDLETON ◆ C. 1570–1627
*A Trick to Catch the Old One*

13. So many goodly cities ransacked and razed; so many nations destroyed and made desolate; so infinite millions of harmless people of all sexes, states and ages massacred, ravaged and put to the sword; and the richest, the fairest, and the best part of the world topsiturvied, ruined and defaced for the traffic of pearls and pepper: Oh, base conquest!

MICHEL EYQUEM DE MONTAIGNE ◆ 1533–1592
*Essays* III

14. There is a dishonour in being overcome by the love of money, or of wealth, or of political power, whether

a man is frightened into surrender by the loss of them, or, having experienced the benefits of money and political corruption, is unable to rise above the seductions of them. For none of these things are of a permanent or lasting nature; not to mention that no generous friendship ever sprang from them.

PAUSANIAS ◆ C. 5TH CENTURY B.C.E.
Quoted in Plato, *Symposium*

15. As for the children of men, they are but vanity: the children of men are deceitful upon the weights, they are altogether lighter than vanity itself. O trust not in wrong and robbery, give not yourselves unto vanity: if riches increase, set not your heart upon them. God spake once, and twice I have also heard the same; that power belongeth unto God; And that thou, Lord, art merciful: for thou rewardest every man according to his work.

*Psalms* 62:9-12

16. O eloquent, just, and mighty Death!...thou hast drawn together all the farstretched greatness, all the pride, cruelty, and ambition of man, and covered it all over with these two narrow words, *Hic jacet.*

WALTER RALEIGH ◆ C. 1552–1618
*A History of the World* V, vi, 12

17. No man has the right to be respected for any other possessions but those of virtue and talents. Titles are tinsel, power a corrupter, glory a bubble, and excessive wealth a libel on its possessor.

PERCY BYSSHE SHELLEY ◆ 1792–1822
*A Declaration of Rights* XXVII

18. A man who raises himself by degrees to wealth and power, contracts, in the course of this protracted labor, habits of prudence and restraint which he cannot afterwards shake off. A man cannot gradually enlarge his mind as he does his house.

> ALEXIS DE TOCQUEVILLE ✦ 1805–1859
> *Democracy in America* 2.3.19

19. Privilege is the greatest enemy of right.

> MARIE VON EBNER-ESCHENBACH ✦ 1830–1916
> *Aphorisms*

# ARGUMENTS FOR THE PURSUIT OF WEALTH AND POWER

20. Those who are not envied are never wholly happy. It is a nobler fate to be envied than to be pitied.

> AESCHYLUS ✦ 525–456 B.C.E.
> *Agamemnon* I

21. As wealth is power, so all power will infallibly draw wealth to itself by some means or other.

> EDMUND BURKE ✦ 1729–1797
> Speech in the House of Commons, February 11, 1780

22. The law may in a mad freak say that all shall have power except the owners of property; they shall have no vote. Nevertheless, by a higher law, the property will, year after year, write every statute that respects property.

> RALPH WALDO EMERSON ✦ 1803–1882
> *Politics*

23. Men, such as they are, very naturally seek money or power; and power because it is as good as money.

RALPH WALDO EMERSON ◆ 1803–1882
*The American Scholar*

24. To the lowly, the powerful and rich are as gods.

EURIPIDES ◆ 485–406 B.C.E.
*Iphigenia in Tauris*

25. Money is power in American politics. It always has been.

WILLIAM GREIDER ◆ 1936–
*Who Will Tell the People*

26. So oblique is human judgment that we nearly always praise the lavish habits of princes, though they be joined with rapacity; more so, in fact, than we praise their parsimony, which is usually attended by a sacred regard for the property of others.

FRANCESCO GUICCIARDINI ◆ 1483–1540
*Storia d'Italia*

27. It is much better to be envied than pitied.

HERODOTUS ◆ C. 485–C. 425 B.C.E.
*Histories*

28. We are . . . removed farther than ever away from the happy sons of earth who lord it over land and sea and men in the full-blown lustihood that wealth and power can give, and before whom, stiffen ourselves as we will by appealing to anti-snobbish first principles,

we cannot escape an emotion, open or sneaking, of
respect and dread.

WILLIAM JAMES ♦ 1842–1910
*Psychology* X

29. Get place and wealth, if possible, with grace;
If not, by any means get wealth and place.

ALEXANDER POPE ♦ 1688–1744
*Imitations of Horace*

## ARGUMENTS AGAINST THE PURSUIT OF WEALTH AND FAME

30. What is fame? an empty bubble;
Gold? a transient, shining trouble.

JAMES GRAINGER ♦ C. 1721–1766
*Solitude* 1.96

## ARGUMENTS AGAINST THE PURSUIT OF WEALTH AND PRAISE

31. Why do we, in fact, almost all of us, desire to increase our incomes? It may seem, at first sight, as
though material goods were what we desire. But, in
fact, we desire these mainly in order to impress our
neighbours. When a man moves into a larger house
in a more genteel quarter, he reflects that "better"
people will call on him and some unprosperous
cronies of former days be dropped. When he sends
his son to a school or an expensive university, he

consoles himself for the heavy fees by thoughts of the kudos to be gained. In every big city, whether of Europe or of America, houses in some districts are more expensive than equally good houses in other districts, merely because they are more fashionable. One of the most powerful of all our passions is the desire to be admired and respected. As things stand, admiration and respect are given to the man who seems to be rich. This is the chief reason why people wish to be rich. The actual goods chased by their money play quite a secondary part.

BERTRAND RUSSELL ♦ 1872–1970
*Sceptical Essays* VI

# ARGUMENTS AGAINST THE PURSUIT OF WEALTH, POWER, AND PLEASURE

32. Avarice is generally the last passion of those lives of which the first part has been squandered in pleasure, and the second devoted to ambition.

SAMUEL JOHNSON ♦ 1709–1784
*The Rambler,* August 27, 1751

33. The boast of heraldry, the pomp of pow'r,
And all that beauty, all that wealth e'er gave,
Awaits alike th' inevitable hour.
The paths of glory lead but to the grave.

THOMAS GRAY ♦ 1716–1771
*Elegy Written in a Country Churchyard*

# ARGUMENTS AGAINST THE FREE PURSUIT OF SEX AND DRINK

34. Kicked into the world a boy without guide or training, or with worse than none, I confess to my shame that few men have drunk deeper of all kinds of sin than I.

> T. H. HUXLEY ◆ 1825–1895
> Letter to Charles Kingsley, September 23, 1860

35. The works of the flesh are manifest, which are these, Adultery, fornication, uncleanness, lasciviousness, idolatry, witchcraft, hatred, variance, emulations, wrath, strife, seditions, heresies, envyings, murders, drunkenness, revellings, and such like.

> SAINT PAUL ◆ 1ST CENTURY
> *Galatians* 5:19-20

36. [L]asciviousness, lusts, excess of wine, revellings, banquetings....

> SAINT PETER ◆ 1ST CENTURY
> *1 Peter* 4:3

37. The disease is the acceptance by the culture of immediate gratification. Abortion, drug abuse, alcoholism, street- and white-collar crime and casual sex are all simply symptoms.

> PAUL MICHAEL WEYRICH ◆ 1942–
> Quoted in *The Washington Post,* May 4, 1986

# ARGUMENTS FOR THE FREE PURSUIT OF SEX AND DRINK

38.  Let us have Wine and Woman, Mirth and Laughter, Sermons and soda-water the day after.

> GEORGE NOEL GORDON, LORD BYRON ◆ 1788–1824
> *Don Juan* 2.178

39.  Fill ev'ry glass, for—wine inspires us, and fires us
With courage, love and joy.
Women and wine should life employ.
Is there ought else on earth desirous?

> JOHN GAY ◆ 1685–1732
> *The Beggar's Opera* II, i, xix

40.  Wine loved I deeply, dice dearly, and in woman outparamoured the Turk.

> WILLIAM SHAKESPEARE ◆ 1564–1616
> *King Lear* III, iv, 84

41.  I am for those who believe in loose delights—I share the midnight orgies of young men; dance with the dancers, and drink with the drinkers.

> WALT WHITMAN ◆ 1819–1892
> *Native Moments*

# INDEX

## A

Abelard, Peter (Pierre
    Abeilard) 135
Acton (John E.E. Dalberg–
    Acton) 43
Adams, Henry 52
Addison, Joseph 43, 103, 129
Adler, Alfred 52
Aeschylus 174
Agassiz, Jean Louis
    Rodolphe 1
Aldrich, Dean 163
Aldrich, Thomas Bailey 32
Allen, Fred (John F. Sullivan)
    81
Amenemope 1
Amiel, Henri Frederic 67,
    169
Anderson, Marian 1
Angelou, Maya 67
Aquinas, Thomas 10, 107
Archilochus 119
Aretino, Pietro 129
Aristotle xv, xxiv, xxxv, 10,
    11, 33, 41, 116

Arnold, Matthew 11
Astor, Nancy 159
Augustine, Saint 12, 53, 90,
    123, 136, 141
Aurelius Antoninus, Marcus
    10, 90, 107
Austen, Jane 32

## B

Bacon, Francis 12, 41, 53, 100
Bagnold, Enid 95, 143
Barr, Amelia E. 12
Barrie, J(ames) M(atthew) 2
Barzini, Luigi 143
Baudelaire, Charles 163
Baum, Vicki 81
Bebel, August 67
Becon, Thomas 159
Bedford, Sybille von
    Schoenebeck 43
Beecher, Henry Ward 113
Behn, Aphra 32, 143
Belloc, Hilaire 32
Bernhardt, Sarah 82

*Bible. See also* Jesus; Saint
  John; Saint Paul; Saint
  Peter
 *2 Samuel* 158
 *Ecclesiastes* 2, 44, 120, 163
 *Ecclesiasticus* (Apocrypha)
  1, 44, 96
 *Genesis* 141
 *Isaiah* 160, 165
 *Job* 2
 *Proverbs* 121, 133, 142, 161,
  166
 *Psalms* 2, 106, 173
Bierce, Ambrose 143
Blake, William 144
Bodeen, DeWitt 2
Boethius (Anicus Manlius
  Severinus Boethius) 12,
  16, 53, 54, 55, 91, 92, 136,
  169, 170
Bohn, Henry George 44, 67
Boileau, Nicolas 92
Bonaparte, Napoleon I 67,
  68, 82
Boswell, James xxi, 33, 128
Browning, Robert 2
Brydges, Sir Edgerton 125
Buchanan, James 44
Buck, Pearl S(ydenstricker)
  3, 103
Buddha (Siddhartha Gau-
  tama) xxii, xxxv, xl, xlii,
  16, 55, 108, 137, 141, 170
Bunyan, John 56
Burke, Edmund 56, 100, 174
Burney, Frances 16
Burns, Robert 144, 170
Bussy–Rabutin, Roger de 68
Butler, Samuel xlviii, 3, 113

Byron, George Noel Gordon,
  Lord xviii, 95, 144, 145,
  163, 179

C

Caesar, Julius 48, 68, 77, 89
Callimachus 130
Campbell, Thomas 44
Camus, Albert 68
Carlyle, Thomas 56, 68, 100,
  101, 108
Carroll, Lewis (Charles Lut-
  widge Dodson) 119
Castillo, Ana 69, 170
Catullus, Gaius Valerius 95,
  145
Cervantes, Miguel de 63, 82
Chanel, Coco (Gabrielle
  Bonheur) 82
Channon, Henry "Chips"
  145
Chapman, George 69
Chaucer, Geoffrey 33, 95,
  130
Cheever, John 130
Christie, Agatha xxiii, 33
Chrysostom, Saint John 56
Churchill, Winston 64
Cicero, Marcus Tullius xx,
  xxx, 64, 101, 128
Clarke, John 69
Coffey, Denise 130
Colton, Charles Caleb 103
Confucius xix, 17, 137
Connolly, Cyril 131, 146
Conrad, Joseph 44
Cooper, James Fenimore 34
Corneille, Pierre 44
Cornuel, Anne Bigot 82

Coryate, Thomas 82
Cowper, William 3
Cromwell, Oliver 104
Cyprian, Saint 56

## D

Dante (Dante Alighieri) 83, 96
Darwin, Charles 125, 146
da Vinci, Leonardo 9
Defoe, Daniel 69
Demarest, Ellen 34
Descartes, René 116
de Gaulle, Charles 126
de Sade, Marquis 151
de Sales, St. Francis 56
Dickinson, Emily 83, 84
Diogenes the Cynic 17
Disraeli, Benjamin 96
Donne, John 131
Dostoevsky, Fyodor Mikhailovich 34, 146
Dryden, John 163

## E

Ebner–Eschenbach, Marie von 174
Edgeworth, Maria 34
Edwards, Richard 147
Einstein, Albert 4
Elizabeth I, Queen 125
Ellis, Havelock 147
Ellison, Ralph 69
Emerson, Ralph Waldo 17, 41, 57, 70, 93, 174, 175
Epictetus xxxv, xxxvii, xxxix, 17, 108, 109, 137, 171

Epicurus xxx, xxxii, xxxv, 18, 57, 93, 137, 171
Erdrich, Louise 4
Euripides 34, 70, 96, 131, 175

## F

Ferber, Edna 147
Fielding, Henry xlvii, 44, 131, 147, 164
Fitzgerald, Edward xv, 45, 164
Flanner, Janet (Genet) 34
Fletcher, John 164
Fletcher, Phineas 147
Ford, Leslie 35
Forster, E(dward) M(organ) 4
Franklin, Benjamin 131, 171
Frederick the Great 120
Freud, Sigmund 138, 155
Fromm, Erich 57
Fuentes, Carlos 147
Fuller, Thomas 4, 70, 83, 113

## G

Galbraith, John Kenneth 35
Gaskell, Elizabeth 104
Gay, John 148, 179
Gibbon, Edward 5, 84, 148, 149
Gibbons, Stella 132
Gide, André 149
Giraudoux, Jean 35, 149
Gissing, George (Robert) 35
Glasgow, Ellen 5
Godwin, William 57
Goethe, Johann Wolfgang von 120

Goldsmith, Oliver 120
Gorky, Maxim (Aleksei
    Peshkov) 45
Gourmont, Remy de 146
Gracián, Baltasar 113
Grainger, James 176
Gray, Thomas 84, 120, 177
Greek Anthology 164
Greene, Graham 85
Greider, William 175
Guicciardini, Francesco 175

**H**

Harris, Sydney Justin 113
Hayes, Helen 85
Heilbrun, Carolyn (Amanda
    Cross) 70
Herbert, George 96
Herodotus 35, 45, 64, 132,
    175
Hillel 5, 85
Hitler, Adolf 71
*Hitopadesa ("Book of Good
    Counsels")* 5, 157
Hobbes, Thomas xii, xv,
    xlviii, 71, 114, 162
Holmes, Oliver Wendell 36,
    71, 85
Holzer, Jenny xviii, 36, 45
Homer 96, 126, 159
Hood, Thomas 121
Horace (Quintus Horatius)
    85, 97, 149, 165
Housman, A(lfred) E(dward)
    126
Howe, E(dgar) W(atson) 36
Huneker, James Gibbons
    149

Huxley, Aldous 58
Huxley, T. H. 178

**J**

James, William 19, 117, 176
Jefferson, Thomas 6, 45, 46,
    86
Jesus xliv, 4, 19, 20, 23, 58,
    59, 93, 109, 172
John, Saint 138
Johnson, Samuel xxi, xxiv,
    36, 37, 104, 128, 165, 177
Jones, El Dorado 72
Jonson, Ben 37, 97
Jung, Carl Gustav 60

**K**

Kant, Immanuel 60
Keats, John xvii, 86, 87, 127
Kempis, Thomas à (Thomas
    Haemerken) 123
Kerr, Jean 6, 160
Khan, Genghis 70
King, Billie Jean 86
Kipling, Rudyard 72, 165
Kirkpatrick, Jeane Jordan 64
*Koran, The* 23
Krafft-Ebing, Richard von
    132
Kronenberger, Louis 86
Kundera, Milan 86

**L**

L'Amour, Louis 97
Lamb, Charles 37, 105
Landor, Walter Savage 105
Lao-tzu 23, 60
Lawrence, D(avid) H(erbert)
    150

La Bruyère, Jean de 46, 114
La Fontaine, Jean de 121
La Rochefoucauld, François, Duc de 37, 105, 114
Lebowitz, Fran 150
Lecky, William E(dward) H(artpole) 132
Leo XIII, Pope 24, 64
Leszcynski, Stanislaus 97
Livy (Titus Livius) 87, 121
Locke, John 60
Longfellow, Henry Wadsworth 72, 97
Lorenz, Konrad 47
Lucretius (Titus Lucretius) 24, 61, 110
Luther, Martin xlvi, 24, 162
Lyly, John 160

**M**

Macaulay, Thomas Babington 127
MacDougall, Alice Foote 72
Machiavelli, Niccolo 61, 72, 114
Mackenzie, George 87
Madonna (Ciccone) 37, 73
Mahan, Alfred Thayer 73
Malcolm X 73
Mansfield, Katherine 37
Mao Tse-Tung 73
Marlowe, Christopher 73, 98
Martial (Marcus Valerius Martialis) 87, 105, 121
Marvell, Andrew 150
Maugham, W(illiam) Somerset 38, 114, 150
May, Rollo 65

McCarthy, Mary 98
Melville, Herman 38
Mencius 25
Mencken, H(enry) L(ouis) 87, 157
Middleton, Thomas 172
Milton, John 74, 98
Mitford, Jessica 160
Monroe, Marilyn 87
Montaigne, Michel Eyquem de xxi, xxx, 25, 61, 93, 94, 110, 117, 123, 124, 155, 156, 172
Montesquieu, Charles de Secondat 61, 117
Moore, Thomas 157
Mordaunt, Thomas Osbert 127
Morell, Thomas 98
Murdoch, Iris 132
Murray, Venetia 157

**N**

Navratilova, Martina 6
Nietzsche, Friedrich Wilhelm 74, 75, 132, 156

**O**

Oates, Joyce Carol 87
Olney, Richard 75
Ovid (Publius Ovidius Naso) 98, 99, 151

**P**

Panchatantra 38
Parker, Dorothy 87, 165
Pascal, Blaise 66, 88, 101, 111, 128

Paul, Saint 25, 139, 178
Pausanias 173
Pepys, Samuel xix, 38, 47
Pericles 38
Perry, Carrie Saxon 66
Persius (Aulus Persius Flaccus) 99
Peter, Saint 139, 178
Petronius, Gaius (Petronius Arbiter) 39, 132
Phelps, Elizabeth Stuart 160
Picasso, Pablo 39
Pindar 106
Pitt, William 47
Plato xii, xxiv, xxxiv, l, 26, 30, 41, 75, 101, 118, 140, 156, 162
Plautus 75
Pliny the Elder (Gaius Plinius Secundus) 166
Pliny the Younger (Gaius Plinius Caecilius Secundus) 6, 99
Plotinus 139
Plutarch 115, 127
Poe, Edgar Allan 47
Poole, Mary Pettibone 160
Pope, Alexander 88, 121, 176
Potter, Eliza 6
Proust, Marcel 151
Proverbs (folk sayings)
  Danish 47
  French 166
  Japanese 106
  Latin 127
  Russian 151
  Sanskrit 99
  Yiddish 166

Publilius Syrus xxviii, 47, 94, 121
Pym, Barbara 142

**Q**

*Qur'an (Koran), The* 23

**R**

Rabutin–Chantal, Marie de (Marquise de Sevigne) 75
Raleigh, Walter 173
Rand, Ayn 39
Repplier, Agnes 133, 161
Ricardo, David 42
Rich, Adrienne 76
Richards, Ellen Henrietta Swallow 76
Robinson, Jill 39
Rockefeller, John D. 39
Roosevelt, Theodore 64, 65
Rossetti, Christina 121
Rousseau, Jean Jacques 26, 111, 112, 118
Rowland, Helen 39
Rudolph, Wilma 88
Rumbold, Richard 48
Ruskin, John 27
Russell, Bertrand xxii, 62, 151, 177

**S**

Sa'di 27
Sadat, Anwar al- 6
Salter, Mary Jo 7
Sand, Georges (Amandine Aurore Lucile Dupin) 7
Sarton, May 89

Schopenhauer, Arthur  27, 42, 112, 118, 140, 156, 157

Seneca, Lucius Annaeus xxxii, 28, 29, 62, 112

Seneca the Younger (Lucius Annaeus Seneca)  161

Service, Robert W.  76

Shakespeare, William  xii, xvi, xvii, xviii, xxv, xxvi, xxxvi, 7, 8, 39, 48, 49, 50, 76, 77, 89, 106, 107, 115, 122, 133, 142, 151, 158, 161, 166, 179

Shaw, George Bernard  65, 134

Shelley, Percy Bysshe  50, 152, 173

Shenstone, William  152

Sheridan, Richard Brinsley  166

Sherman, W(illiam) T(ecumseh)  50

Silius Italicus  126

Skutch, Alexander Frank  29

Smart, Elizabeth  152

Smith, Adam  29

Smith, Logan Pearsall  8

Smith, Sydney  122

Socrates  xxxiv, 30, 140

Sophocles  127

Solzhenitsyn, Alexander  30

Spinoza, Baruch  xxxvi, xxxix, 30, 95, 125, 141

Stalin, Joseph (Josif Vissarionovich Dzhugashvili)  77

Stein, Gertrude  8, 40

Steinem, Gloria  77, 78

Steiner, George  153

Stendhal (Marie Henri Beyle)  153

Stevenson, Robert Louis  8

Stewart, Mary  51

Stirner, Max  78

Stravinsky, Igor  89

**T**

Tacitus, (Cornelius)  51, 99

Tagore, Rabindranath  63, 112

Taylor, John  134

Teenage Mother  134

Tennyson, Alfred, Lord  78

Tertullian (Quintus Septimius)  31

Thatcher, Margaret  xix, 40

Theognis  31

Theroux, Paul  89

Thomas, Dylan  167

Thompson, Frank, Jr.  153

Thoreau, Henry David  xxxix, 31

Tocqueville, Alexis de  174

Tolstoy, Leo Nikolaevich  8, 63, 153

Trilling, Diana  162

Truman, Harry S.  51

Truth, Sojourner  51

Tucker, Benjamin R.  78

Tucker, Sophie  40

Twain, Mark (Samuel Langhorne Clemens)  8, 40, 154

## V

Vanbrugh, John  158
Vegetius (Flavius Vegetius
     Renatus)  65
Vidal, Gore  52, 134
Virgil (Publius Vergilius
     Maro)  100
Vogelweide, Walther von
     der  79
Voltaire (François Marie
     Arouet)  42, 79, 89, 158

## W

Walker, Margaret  9
Walpole, Horace  52
Waugh, Evelyn  9
Webster, John  90, 122
Weinstein, Paula  52
Weyrich, Paul Michael  178

Wharton, Edith  40
Whitman, Walt  154, 179
Wilde, Oscar (Fingall
     O'Flahertie Wills)  154
Wilder, Thornton  9
Williams, Tennessee (Thom-
     as Lanier)  155
Wilson, Barbara  134
Wilson, Bishop Thomas  112
Wollstonecraft, Mary  9, 66
Woolf, Virginia  40

## X

Xenophon  115

## Y

Young, Edward  52

## Z

Zaharias, Babe Didrikson
     100

# ACKNOWLEDGMENTS AND PERMISSIONS

Niccolo Machiavelli, *The Prince*, translated by W.K. Marriott, reprinted by permission of Everyman's Library.

Epictetus, *Fragments*, translated by Robin Hard, reprinted by permission of Everyman's Library.

Blaise Pascal, *Pensées*, translated by W.F. Trotter, reprinted by permission of Everyman's Library.

Boethius, *The Consolation of Philosophy*, translated by V. E. Watts (Penguin, 1969), copyright © 1969 by V. E. Watts. Reproduced by permission of Penguin Books, Ltd.

*The Dhammapada (The Path of Perfection)*, translated by Juan Mascaro (Penguin, 1973), copyright © 1973 by Juan Mascaro. Reproduced by permission of Penguin Books, Ltd.

St. Augustine, *Confessions*, translated by Frank Sheed and published by Sheed & Ward.

Thomas Aquinas, *Summa Theologica*, published by Christian Classics.

Noël Coward, *Poor Little Rich Girl*, published by Methuen Publishing Limited, Copyright © 1984 by the Estate of Noël Coward.

Aristotle, *Ethics*, translated by W.D. Ross; Aristotle, *Politics and Economics*, translated by B. Jowett; Aristotle, *Rhetoric and Poetics*, translated by W. Rhys Roberts, from the Oxford Translation of Aristotle edited by W.D. Ross, reprinted by permission of Oxford University Press.

*The Complete Essays of Montaigne*, translated by Donald M. Frame, copyright © 1958 by the Board of Trustees of the Leland Stanford Junior University. Used with the permission of Stanford University Press, www.sup.org.